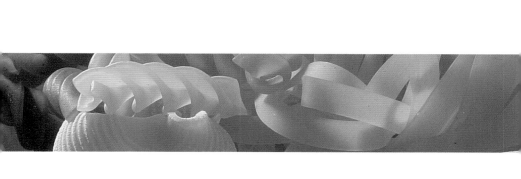

LEXICON OF

PASTA

A little declaration of love

by

Tobias Pehle and Birgit Andrich

© 2005 Rebo International b.v., Lisse, The Netherlands

This 2nd edition reprinted in 2006.

Author: Tobis Pehle & Birgit Andrich
Typesetting: AdAm Studio, Prague, The Czech Republic
Translator: Andrew Brown for First Edition Translations Ltd,
Cambridge, UK
Editor: Sally Heavens for First Edition Translations Ltd
Proofreading: Sarah Dunham

ISBN 13: 978-90-366-1889-2
ISBN 10: 90-366-1889-4

Contents

Preface

ENJOY READING, ENJOY EATING!

Yet another pasta cookbook? No! This is not a standard cookbook with endless pasta recipes—nor is it trying to be. There are hundreds of those around already.

Rather, this is a book about pasta: a short and succinct declaration of love for Italian pasta cooking. It includes a great deal of information about pasta: its significance in the *cucina italiana* and culinary history, the production and varieties of pasta, classic dishes that are prized worldwide, and the regional specialties that are no less remarkable. This is a book aimed at all lovers of pasta cooking—and at those who would like to become so enamored. The reader will find here much more than cookbooks usually have to offer: for instance, a wealth of basic information on cooking in the different regions of Italy, from the Alpine north to the southernmost tip of Italy's "boot." We provide fundamental information on, for example, the perfect way to cook *pasta al dente*, or making pasta cases at home. And our book is arranged like a work of reference, making it easy to look up any information on pasta quickly and easily: for instance, the exact nature of *ragiatoni* or *fussili*.

You will of course find all the essential recipes here—from making a *pesto* sauce to layering a lasagna. These and other classic recipes are supplemented by dishes from Italy's individual regions—meals that count among the country's culinary highlights.

These dishes have been selected to cater for every taste (and pocket): quick and easy-to-prepare *tagliatelle al prosciutto* (pasta with ham), lavish fish dishes such as *pasta con le sarde*, and gourmet variants such as *fettucini* with white truffles. Brief insets next to the dishes offer practical help to the reader. They present the most important details:

Pasta

75 min.

- COOKING TIME: this is given in minutes, next to the hourglass symbol.

- DIFFICULTY: the saucepans tell you how labor-intensive the dish is to cook. One saucepan means "easy," two saucepans means "a bit more demanding," and three saucepans means "more difficult."

- COST: the piles of coins give guidance on the price of ingredients, ranging from one pile (inexpensive) to three piles (expensive).

- CALORIES: the nutritional value of the dish is indicated in tomatoes—from one tomato, meaning "light fare," to three tomatoes, or "heavy fare."

Italian pasta:
Local flavor

PASTA—THE EPITOME OF ITALY

For people from central, northern, and eastern Europe, the well-known taste of pasta always reminds them of their holidays: the sun of southern Europe, the atmosphere of romantic cities, and dolce far niente—all of this is conjured up when you open your senses to the heart of *la cucina italiana*, Italian cuisine.

The incomparable aroma that spreads from the kitchen as soon as you start cooking in olive oil, the wonderful color combinations formed when red tomatoes, green basil, and white garlic come together, and the way you can tickle your taste-buds by sampling the *pesto*, *salsa*, or *sugo* (juice) all prove that the pasta-lover has not only an Italian palate, but also an Italian heart.

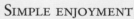

SIMPLE ENJOYMENT

So, with just a few inexpensive ingredients, even if you do not have much experience of cooking you can quickly and easily take a short break from the hectic schedule of everyday life and transport yourself into a delightful culinary world.

Herein, no doubt, lies one of the most fundamental reasons why pasta enjoys such great popularity worldwide. Italy stands for a way of life in which you can find satisfaction in simple, traditional things, rather than over-sophisticated, complicated, and demanding ones.

A simple stove with spaghetti cooking on it, an old wooden table with rustic tableware, a few fresh olives and tomatoes, with olive oil and balsamic vinegar—you do not need much more than this to cut yourself a slice of happiness.

It seems perfectly apt that it is not the choice specialties that are the pasta dishes prized most highly worldwide, but rather the simple recipes such as pasta with *pesto genovese* or *salsa pomodori*. This becomes especially clear if we contrast it with the second great national cuisine of Europe, that of France.

When you think of French cooking, you think of sophisticated dishes such as *coque au vin* or *petits fours*, of magnificently laid tables in exclusive restaurants, and of internationally renowned chefs who can create real works of art.

It is quite different in Italian cuisine. Here you find simple pasta dishes, lovingly prepared by an Italian *mamma* in a cozy pizzeria round the corner.

These images and the culinary worlds that they represent could scarcely be more different and more striking—despite the fact that both nations work predominantly with the same ingredients.

IRRESISTIBLE TASTE

Of course, pasta cookery can also offer sophisticated delicacies of great subtlety. And it goes without saying that in Italy, too, internationally celebrated chefs can conjure up sensational dishes, the products of vivid imagination, great skill, and the most refined ingredients such as truffles or quails. In the final analysis, however, it is, yet again, not the star chefs who define the characteristics of pasta cookery, but the simple, traditional meals.

So it is also fitting that many connoisseurs prefer to enjoy their favorite pasta almost pure—with just a little olive oil and a dash of garlic, or with butter and freshly grated parmesan. The fact that these simple dishes can become real culinary experiences stems from the quality of the pasta. The simpler the basic recipe of the dough (all you need is flour, salt, and eggs), the more delicious your pasta will taste.

COOKING WITH NATURAL RESOURCES

The most beautiful things around us are made of the simplest natural materials, such as wood or stone. The fact that it is in particular the Italians who, for thousands of years, have created the most precious things from these materials is the result of the wealth of natural resources that their country holds—you need think only of the white marble of Carrara, from which the world's most beautiful statues have been carved.

The same is true of Italian cuisine. It too, would be unthinkable without the natural wealth found in Italy, washed as it is by the waves of the Mediterranean. Be it fruit or vegetables, meat or fish—the choice is simply enormous.

And it is this plethora of the most varied ingredients that explains the several hundred pasta dishes that, over the centuries, have been invented and developed from the Southern Alps to Sicily.

Furthermore, the different traditions of cooking and eating in individual regions have always been reflected in the variety of pasta dishes. What would the pasta meals from the region around Parma be without the city's eponymous, world-famous ham? And what would the pasta dishes of the coastal regions be without the *vongole* (mussels) or *frutti di mare* (seafood) found in such abundance in the Mediterranean?

A MIRROR OF ITALY

The different pasta dishes in all their multiplicity thus reflect the different faces of Italy, creating a picture that is as enthralling as it is varied—and one of more than just Italian culinary culture. They also highlight the landscape, the prevailing agricultural economy, and even the mentality of the people. So it is certainly no coincidence if the subtly devised taste of pesto was invented in Genoa, once a world-class city. In the period of its brilliance the best chefs not only of Italy, but of the entire world, worked in its kitchens.

On the other hand, *ragù bolognese* from Emila-Romagna, or *pasta alla romagna* from Latium, both of which are made from the simplest ingredients, point to peasant origin. Such dishes use only ingredients that grow in the kitchen gardens of these regions. They thus mirror the simple lifestyle of an economically poor environment.

QUICK AND EASY TO PREPARE

Whichever region of Italy you look at, the picture is the same: pasta is cooked everywhere, in all social classes, in every age group, and in every type of social structure. Pasta is indissolubly linked with Italian family life. And the reason for this, too, is easy to find: you can cook pasta in great quantities very cheaply and easily. All you need—apart from more pasta—is a bigger saucepan. Furthermore, you can cook pasta very quickly. It is ready in just a few minutes.

So these days in particular, when even cooking generally needs to be done quickly and easily, pasta offers a practical alternative to lavish recipes.

And it is unbelievably easy to cook pasta: bring salted water to the boil, throw in the pasta—and in a few minutes, spaghetti, tortellini, and company are ready to be served. That is all it takes. Admittedly, preparing a really nice sauce to go with it is somewhat trickier. But even a novice cook can whip up a simple tomato sauce without too much difficulty. The fact that it is so quick and easy to prepare is another significant reason why pasta is such a worldwide success.

COOKING WITH ENJOYMENT AND CREATIVITY

You will, of course, only really enjoy cooking pasta if you devote time and love to it. The reason does not lie simply in the hundreds of different ways of making up a sauce. It is really the pasta itself that is the source of fascination, for the eyes as much as for the palate, in its huge variety of form and color. Simple spirals (fussili), little nest shapes (fettucini), and artfully folded butterflies (farfalle)—Italian cuisine knows over 300 varieties of pasta. And every day there are more of them: throughout the world, pasta design is an art in itself—one that does not stop short of the wackiest ideas, such as football pasta shaped like boots or balls. This huge range of possibilities simply invites you to give free range to your own creativity when cooking pasta. Hardly any other type of cooking makes it possible to develop your very own taste in the way that pasta cookery does: the selection of pasta, the invention of sauce recipes, and the way you lay your table, are all yours to choose.

Pasta is good for you and makes you happy—so they say in Italy. And it has indeed been scientifically proven that pasta is not fattening.

In fact, pasta plays an important role in the nutrition of sportsmen and sportswomen, especially in sports that demand stamina. In balanced combination with additional ingredients, pasta can be a source of healthy nourishment.

Pasta is good for you

The secret of pasta lies in the dough. If you compare the contents of pasta all'uovo (made with eggs), pasta secca (dry pasta), and pasta integrale (whole-wheat pasta), the latter naturally comes off best when it comes to providing roughage. Pasta made with eggs or whole-wheat flour also contains more minerals than pasta made from semolina. But this alone does not make one sort of pasta healthier than the other. What is lacking in one sort of pasta can easily be made up for by a suitable combination with other ingredients. Adding vegetables, for instance, can increase the roughage of pasta dishes. And leaving out cheese, creamy sauces, and additional eggs can keep the cholesterol level of a meal of egg-based pasta within acceptable limits.

Generally speaking, pasta with vegetables constitutes an optimally nutritious combination; furthermore, it limits the intake of protein and fat.

Indeed, while pasta consists of 70 percent carbohydrates, it has comparatively few calories—on average, 350 calories per 3½oz (100 g) of uncooked pasta. The proportion of fat is small, and even with the addition of eggs is only slightly increased. Combining the pasta with vegetables and cheese can increase its predominantly vegetable protein content, which is around 15 percent.

Pasta contains almost exclusively complex carbohydrates that are only slowly broken down by the body. It thus provides an outstanding source of slow-release energy for physical and mental work. Pasta also increases concentration. In addition, whole-wheat pasta contains roughage—carbohydrates that are

unusable as energy, but provide bulk and facilitate digestion. In whole-wheat pasta, this proportion can be as high as 8 percent.

Certain vitamins can also be found in pasta. In egg-based pasta there is valuable vitamin A, and in whole-wheat pasta we find the B vitamins. Pasta also contains potassium, magnesium, and iron.

On top of all that—pasta really does make you happy! And not just because it tastes good. The complex carbohydrates play a large part in the process, since the body relies on carbohydrates in order to build up the happiness hormone, serotonin. These carbohydrates in turn require protein building blocks such as the amino acid tryptophan, found in animal products, for their transport around the body. *Pasta fresca* and *pasta secca* with a cream sauce and cheese contain both, and thus contribute to a good mood. What could be healthier?

THE QUALITY OF PASTA

Is it quite indisputable that the health value of pasta is high, but it is worth taking a closer look when you buy the ingredients. Even if the differences in the content of pasta are small, there are variations in quality.

You can recognize good-quality pasta from its smooth surface and uniform color. Most of the original Italian pasta products from the few traditional factories are generally of good quality.

ORGANICALLY PRODUCED PASTA

Of course, organic pasta—whether made from whole-wheat or semolina—has certain advantages over the standard products. Its ingredients have fewer residues, being carefully produced in ecologically controlled conditions without the addition of pesticides and inorganic fertilizers.

Egg-based organic pasta contains eggs that are laid by free-range hens. Since all organic products are freshly processed, the nutrients are to a large extent preserved. No use is made of artificial additives such as color, flavoring, and preservatives. This is also true of filled, colored, and flavored pasta. Here too, only organically produced ingredients are used.

AN OVERVIEW OF NUTRITIONAL VALUES

The exact nutritional value of individual pasta dishes varies with the mode of preparation and quality of ingredients. The following list can thus give just basic guidance.

CONTENTS OF 3½ OZ (100G) EGG-BASED PASTA:

Contents	Uncooked	Cooked
Kcal	362	145
KJ	1513	606
Water	12%	65%
Protein	13%	6.2%
Fat	2.8%	1.1%
Carbohydrates	71.2%	28.5%
Roughage	approx. 1%	0.4%
Vitamin A	63 IU	25.2 IU
Vitamin E	300 IU	120 IU
Vitamin B1	170 IU	68 IU
Vitamin B2	73 IU	29.2 IU
Sodium	17mg	6.8mg
Potassium	164mg	66.5mg
Magnesium	67mg	26.8mg
Calcium	27mg	10.8mg
Iron	1.6mg	0.6mg
Phosphorus	191mg	76.4mg
Fluorine	80mg	32mg
Linol acid	830mg	332mg
Linolen acid	76mg	30.4mg

MOST IMPORTANT CONTENTS OF 3½ OZ (100G) OF PASTA WITHOUT EGGS:

Contents	Uncooked	Cooked
Kcal	354	143
KJ	1484	599
Water	13%	65%
Protein	10.2%	4.1%
Fat	0.9%	0.59%
Carbohydrates	1.4%	28.2%
Roughage	0.9%	1,1%
Vitamin A	0 IU	0 IU
Vitamin E	1780 IU	720 IU
Vitamin B1	100 IU	40 IU
Vitamin B2	30 IU	10 IU
Sodium	380mg	150mg
Potassium	100mg	40mg
Magnesium	31mg	12mg
Calcium	21mg	10mg
Iron	1mg	0.44mg
Phosphorus	99mg	43mg
Fluorine	100mg	40mg
Linol acid	830mg	250mg
Linolen acid	76mg	10mg

The history of pasta

A LONG HISTORY

To no other foodstuff do Italians devote such love and care as they do to their pasta. And that has always been the case. Throughout Italy's long, and often stormy, history pasta was (and still is) quite simply the food of the people.

THE ETRUSCANS WERE ALREADY EATING PASTA

Several centuries before the Common or Christian Era (B.C.E.) the inhabitants of the Italian peninsula were already eating pasta. Indeed, pasta was their basic foodstuff.

This, at least, is what some reliefs on an Etruscan grave from the 4th century B.C.E. in Cerveteri, north of Rome, indicate. Together with other cooking utensils, here are depicted several implements that were quite possibly used in pasta production. They include a *rotella dentata* or little wheel for cutting dough, very similar to our present-day utensil. But there is more evidence too: the Roman writers Horace and Cicero for instance were great lovers of *lagani* (thin strips of dough made of flour and water) that were clearly the forerunners of today's lasagna.

Many of Italy's most wonderful and nutritious meals have survived unchanged across the centuries. Pasta is one of them. Horace enjoyed eating it with leeks and chickpeas, with *lasagna e ceci* (lasagna with chickpeas) still remaining a popular dish in the southern region of Basilicata.

THE FIRST COOKBOOKS

We even find several pasta recipes in one of the first cookbooks, compiled by the Roman gastronome Apicius, in 25 B.C.E. There is one, for instance, which gives details of how to make a lasagna in clear soup, and another for a timballo, a sweet and spicy kind of confection that included pasta as one of its ingredients. Later, in medieval texts, we find several references to macaroni. In Boccaccio's short story "Calandrino" there is an enthusiastic hymn of culinary praise in honor of macaroni and cheese—a meal of great simplicity that is still universally enjoyed today. In the first collection of Renaissance recipes from the 15th century, the compiler Maestro Martino da Corno gives precise instructions for making vermicelli and drying it in the sun.

A hundred or so years later, Bartolomeo Scappi included another pasta recipe in his famous "Opera," one that has with good reason remained unchanged to the present day: *tagliatelle*. On the basis of these and other documents from the next two centuries (in every case composed by the cooks of the ruling houses and nobility of the time), we can deduce that pasta had also become the food of the wealthy and privileged.

On their tables, you could find pasta in the form of *pasticci*—huge casseroles of macaroni, meat, fish, vegetables, spices, and sweet ingredients that were often baked in a dough wrapping. Scappi included over a dozen of these heavy pasta casseroles in his menu for a Renaissance feast: they contained, among other ingredients, goat's meat, sweetbread, hare, quail, calf's tongue, trout, and turtle.

A general movement in favor of pasta began toward the end of the 18th century in the southern region of Campania. Not only was the soil here ideal for growing the durum wheat from which pasta is produced, but also the climate was suitable for drying it out, due in no small part to the sea breezes around Naples.

THE FIRST PASTA FACTORIES

The first pasta factories were built in the south of the country in the 19th century. Hard durum wheat was ground to semolina in great hand-mills of granite. To the rhythmic chimes of the mandolin, men and children then kneaded the dough with their bare feet in giant troughs. Finally, primitive machines were used to cut out the pasta shapes, which were dried on long racks.

These days, pasta is made in factories in almost every region of Italy and exported worldwide. It will come as no surprise to learn that big Italian combines are market leaders in the international pasta business and maintain subsidiary companies around the globe.

PASTA AND POLITICS

Pasta has even played a role in Italian politics. For instance, the Futurists, who at the start of the 20th century delighted in assailing traditions of every kind, found the national passion for pasta an ideal target for their attacks. In 1932 the writer Filippo Marinetti published his manifesto "La Cucina Futurista". In it, he mocked pasta as an absurd "gastronomic religion" of Italy and called for it to be "annihilated." Clearly, his compatriots paid little heed to his demands: they simply devoured ever-greater quantities of pasta.

Dough: all you need to know

PASTA MEANS DOUGH

The word "pasta" simply means "dough" and refers to the mixture of water, flour, and salt, usually with eggs and oil, from which it is made. In some types of pasta, semolina is used as the basic ingredient. From this basic mixture, the most varied types of pasta are shaped, all of them with their individual names—spaghetti, tagliatelle, penne, and farfalle.

There is a widespread belief that Italian pasta is generally made without eggs, but this is incorrect. There are plenty of

recipes for egg-based pasta in Italy—one need only think of the delicious *pasta fatta a casa*, the homemade pasta still served today, at least on Sundays and special occasions. It often includes several eggs. In Italy itself there is not just one, universal pasta recipe, but also many distinguishable variants. For example, in every region there is a traditional local variant of dough.

Pasta fresca and pasta secca

In the preparation of the absolutely innumerable different pasta dishes, a basic distinction is drawn between two types of pasta. You can either choose *pasta fresca* (fresh pasta) or *pasta secca* (dry pasta). Both types are found in abundance, varying not just in their countless different shapes, but above all in the way they are made and how they taste.

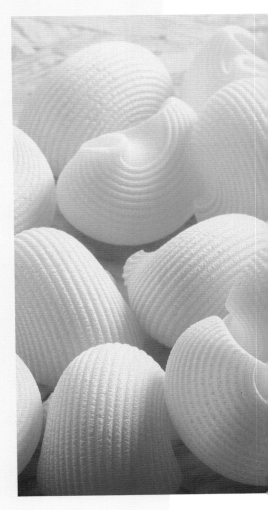

Pasta fresca

PASTA LEGENDS

In Italy there are many wonderful legends about the rise of the classical pasta dishes. For instance, it is said that one particular type of pasta was invented by the Bolognese chef Cristoforo di Zeffirano on the occasion of the wedding of Alfonso d'Este and Lucrezia Borgia in 1503. The young bride's golden locks are supposed to have inspired the master chef to develop tagliatelle. Most of these entertaining stories, however, are simply flights of fancy—the real facts are generally more sober and less interesting.

VERSE PASTA

Literally, *pasta fresca* means "fresh pasta." This type is mainly made in northern Italy— traditionally from plentiful eggs, flour, salt, and olive oil. But it is also prepared in central Italy, though here fewer eggs (or none at all) are the rule. Southern Italy, finally, is the home of pasta made from semolina and water—a kind that is enjoying worldwide popularity at the moment.

But whether it is northern, southern, or central Italy we are talking about, every family has its own recipe for *pasta fresca*, which is a mainstay of centuries-old family traditions.

PASTA LISCIA AND PASTA RIPIENA

Pasta fresca is divided into two main sorts: *pasta liscia* (smooth, flat pasta) and *pasta ripiena* (filled pasta), in which the dough is molded into various shapes and filled with a range of delicious ingredients.

In some kinds of *pasta liscia*, such as *tagliatelle* (wide strips of *pasta fresca*) or *taglierini* (thin strips of *pasta fresca*), the name is derived from the Italian verb *tagliare* (to cut), since these pastas are produced by slicing up a thin layer of dough.

Pasta liscia is also found in the shape of big rectangles (such as the lasagna of Liguria, i.e., as big as a handkerchief) or narrow rectangles (such as the *maccheroni alla chitarra* from Abruzzo). This latter type is generally made with a special implement that has strings like those of a guitar, which are used to cut the pasta.

But the other kind of *pasta fresca*, i.e., *pasta ripiena* (filled pasta), has brought out the creative powers of many a cook over the centuries, with the dough being cut, filled, and folded in increasingly innovative, highly imaginative shapes.

This kind of pasta is very widespread in northern and central Italy, while it is very rarely found in the south, since in earlier times people did not have enough eggs to make the dough

malleable enough to be kneaded into shapes that could be filled.

Dough cases for filling

The best known and most popular dough cases are the little, square ones called ravioli. This kind of pasta can contain a great number of different ingredients, and comes in an incredible range of varieties.

Agnolotti from Piedmont are squares with wavy edges and a filling of meat and cabbage; *agnolini* from Emilia Romagna are crescents filled with meat and vegetables; and *tortelli* are somewhat bigger square cases filled with spinach and ricotta—very popular in central Italy.

The smallest are *cappelletti*, looped dough from Bologna containing a nourishing mix of pork, chicken or turkey, mortadella, ham, parmesan, and nutmeg. *Cappelletti* are very versatile and can be served with a butter or cream sauce or in a clear soup (a traditional meal for Christmas Eve). One romantic but probably apocryphal story claims that *cappelletti* take their shape from a woman's navel.

Pasta secca

DRY PASTA

Pasta secca originated in southern Italy. It was in particular the region around Naples that offered the best conditions for the production of this type of pasta.

Wind and weather were at their most favorable here, enabling huge quantities of spaghetti to be hung out to dry on washing lines in the open air. In addition to this, only here was the special kind of durum wheat found from which pasta was originally made. It is therefore indisputable that the southern Italians were the first to discover pasta.

Gradually, however, pasta pursued its triumphant progress northward, with pasta recipes starting to vary from one region to another. These days, thousands of tons of *pasta secca* are produced every day by manufacturers in every corner of the world. The time when *pasta secca* was produced in Italian households on a homemade basis is long gone.

Naples was in bygone days famous for its *pasta secca*, which was hung out to dry in the streets,

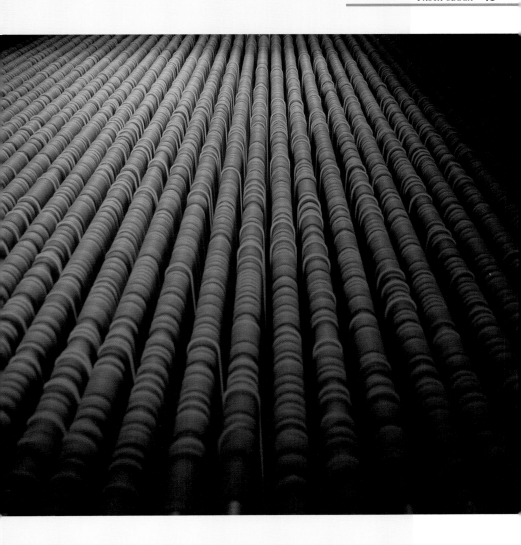

a permanent feature that looked rather like long rows of curtains. Health and hygiene standards require that pasta be treated rather differently these days, so its production is now almost entirely industrial. Manufacturers predominantly use expensive semolina (without eggs) for the dough, with the desired shapes being punched out by machines.

This pasta is then dried in automatic devices and sometimes (in the case of smaller, top-quality producers) in special chambers, in which the pasta remains for two days.

These days, the drying of really high-quality *pasta secca* has become completely automated: a constant temperature of between 60 and 70 degrees is required over a period of 15 hours.

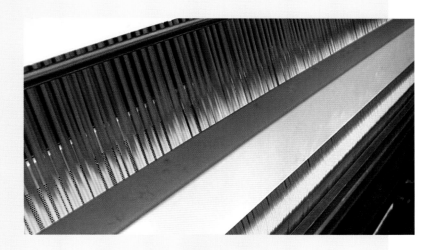

Strips of long pasta, *pasta lunga* (e.g., spaghetti), are hung out to dry next to one another, on long iron poles. But short pasta, *pasta corta*, is, after drying, placed on a conveyor belt on which it is thoroughly shaken. Only in this way can the individual strands of pasta be separated from one another.

Spaghetti—a long history

We can trace the precursors of spaghetti back as far as the 12th century. According to one Arab researcher, a type of pasta named tria ("little strings") was already being produced in Sicily at that time: it was wound round knitting needles to give it its shape. This was none other than what we now know of as spaghetti.

Pasta: a short ABC

300 DIFFERENT TYPES OF PASTA

Thick or thin, round or square, long or short: there are over 300 types of pasta in Italian cuisine, all of them different in shape, size, and color.

There is, furthermore, hardly any attractive shape that the Italians have not immortalized in the form of pasta: sea-shells, stars, snails, croissants, and even little ears. The range of pasta is huge and varied.

Italian *pasta secca*, mainly produced industrially even in Italy, is found in every conceivable shape and form. It would naturally require a lot of time and effort to reproduce these shapes in homemade pasta.

SHAPE AND TASTE

Italian cooks are never faced with the difficult predicament of having to choose which of an incredible variety of shapes and sizes to use for a particular dish. In the homeland of pasta there are strict rules for this. You just know that a simple sauce of olive oil and garlic goes best with spaghetti.

For a *ragù alla bolognese* you need slender ribbon pasta, but a pungent hare ragout will be tastiest with broad ribbon pasta. Why this should be so can never, of course, be definitively explained. One reason may lie in the fact that different pasta shapes are able to absorb different amounts of sauce. There is, for example, no question that penne have more storage capacity, so to speak, than spaghetti. But the type of surface involved is also important. More sauce will invariably stick to fine-grooved varieties of pasta (*rigata*) than smooth pasta (*liscia*). For soups and stews, on the other hand, the small or medium-sized kinds of pasta are more suitable.

PASTA FROM A TO Z

This is in no way meant to be a comprehensive list of every type of pasta, but just a quick overview of the commonest pasta shapes. The name and appearance of pasta can vary with region and manufacturer.

■ AGNOLOTTI: square or rectangular dough cases filled with cheese, meat, or poultry.

■ ANELLI: rings of pasta, suitable for various dishes.

■ ANELLINI: small rings, mostly used in soups.

■ ANOLINI: small, filled, crescent-shaped pasta cases, mostly served in clear soups.

■ BAVETTE AND BAVETTINE: slender ribbon pasta, originally from Genoa. Of all the types of long, semolina-based pasta, *bavette* is especially suitable for allowing the taste of the sauce to develop. The sauce gets trapped in the twists and turns of the pasta, with all its flavorsome variety then being released onto the tongue. *Bavette* and *bavettine* remain firm to the bite even in thinner, runnier sauces.

■ BIGOLI: thick spaghetti of whole-wheat flour.

■ BUCCATINI: thin tubes of pasta, about as long as spaghetti, but with a bigger diameter. This pasta's consistency and hollowness, and the way it stays perfectly firm in cooking, makes it an ideal basis for thick, highly-flavored sauces. *Buccatini* is of ancient origin and comes from central Italy. In particular, it was so popular in the region around Rome that in the course of time it became synonymous with Italian cuisine. *Buccatini* is especially suitable for the strong, intense tastes of dishes in the peasant tradition.

■ CANNELLONI: thick tubes of pasta, for filling. Cannelloni was already known in ancient times. In early days it was prepared from water, wheat, and salt; cut into big, rectangular pieces; filled and rolled up; and only then cooked. Since it retains its firmness when cooked, and has a lot of room inside for fillings, cannelloni is ideal for the richest and most exquisite dishes of traditional Italian cuisine. It is even a distinctive sight when laid out on a plate. The large capacity of cannelloni really cries out for an imaginative filling.

■ CAPELLINI: long threads of pasta (like vermicelli), looking like angels' hair; good for light sauces and fish dishes.

- CAPPELLI D'ANGELO: delicate nests of vermicelli.

- CAPPELLETTI: small, hat-shaped pieces of filled pasta.

- CASERECCE: twisted pasta, from the famous culinary traditions of Sicily. *Caserecce* has a peculiar rolled-up shape, reminiscent of ancient rolls of parchment. The smooth, porous surface means that delicate vegetable sauces can gradually release their flavors to the maximum degree.

- CAVATELLI: a somewhat rare kind of pasta, reminiscent of peas or beans that have burst open.

- CELLENTANI: small pieces of pasta in the shape of curls of hair.

- CONCHIGLIE: shell-shaped pasta of various sizes— large for ample lashings of sauce, small for soups. It looks

like shells from the seabed and is probably one of the most famous and popular types of pasta in the world. Grooved on the outside, the structure (with plenty of space tucked away inside, able fully to absorb even those sauces that do not stick) makes it a real masterpiece.

COTELLI/CAVATAPPI: corkscrews.

- CRESTE DI GALLO: rooster's combs.

- DITALI: unfilled, small, hat-shaped pasta.

- DITALINI: little thimbles of pasta.

- ELICHE: spirals of pasta, able to absorb the taste of more delicate sauces very effectively.

- ELICHE TRICOLORI: spirals in three colors.

- FAGOTTINI: little cases of filled pasta.

■ FARFALLE: the Italian word for butterflies. *Farfalle* is the variant of an ancient sort of pasta that was produced in Emilia Romagna. A square piece of dough was pressed together in the middle of the hand. The delicate, vibrant shape is reminiscent of a butterfly, while the glowing yellow color reminds one of ripe wheat and southern sunshine. The pasta is cut into squares and gently gathered in the middle to make it a little thicker, but the wings remain thinner and lighter. *Farfalle* is mainly served with the most subtle vegetable and fish dishes.

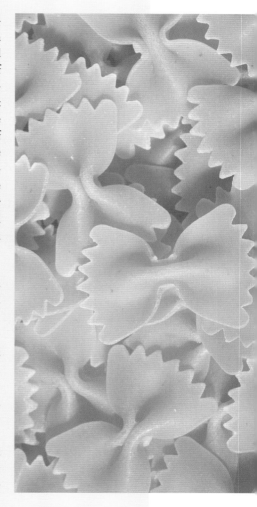

■ FARFALLE TRICOLORI: butterfly-shaped pasta in three colors—particularly suitable for very decorative recipes.

■ FARFALLINE: small, butterfly-shaped pasta for soups.

■ FEDILINI: a type of vermicelli, often used in soups.

■ FETTUCCINE: ribbon pasta rolled into nests; fettuccine is made of wide, flat strands of pasta dough, that while

still uncooked are molded into neat little nest shapes. During preparation, these pasta nests open up and fill the plate with their attractive shapes.

Fettuccine is made from rough, porous dough and is always firm to the bite. Since it helps the different tastes to develop in the mouth, it is perfect for absorbing the many different sauces of Italian cuisine.

■ FUSILLI: spirals, short when used for stews and long for tomato sauces. *Fusilli* first appeared in its current form in southern Italy and originally derived from the idea of winding spaghetti onto a knitting needle. Only later, as a result of the varied tastes customarily found in the different Italian regions, did *fusilli* develop into an independent type of pasta that can now be obtained anywhere in the world. *Fusilli* is equally suitable for expensive meals and simple sauces.

■ FUSILLI LUNGHI: long, spiral pasta.

■ GARGANELLI: short pasta tubes.

- GEMELLI: two strands of pasta twisted together. The name *gemelli*, meaning "twins," indicates one of the original characteristics of this type of pasta: the twin shape. The structure of *gemelli*, with its double twist of pasta threads, is reminiscent of the spiral shape of *fusilli*. This "design" gives *gemelli* a particular consistency. It remains firm to the bite; the shape is exceptionally good at absorbing the different tastes combined in a sauce.

- GIRANDOLE: spiral pasta that goes well with sauces of cream and butter.

- GNOCCHI: these well-known dumplings have a particular place among Italian pasta specialties, since they are produced from potato dough. Dried gnocchi made of semolina are similar only in appearance to potato-based pasta. You can enjoy classic gnocchi like pasta, accompanying every type of *salsa* and *sugo* (juice), and they are especially popular in soups—especially tomato soup.

- LASAGNA: broad, rectangular pasta cases of rough, porous dough, especially good for casseroles. The recipe for lasagna comes from the Emilia-Romagna region. This was also the place where thinly rolled egg dough (known as *sfoglia*) originated.

- LINGUINE: thin ribbon pasta.

- LUMACHE: pasta shaped like a snail-shell, good for tomato sauces.

- MACARONI: long, thick cylindrical pasta: one of the classics of Italian pasta cookery. It is used with rich sauces and casseroles. Here too there are several, very different variants—from broader, longer cylinders to shorter, thinner designs.

- MAFALDINE: long ribbon pasta with a wavy edge, that keeps its shape even after cooking. The secret of this pasta lies in a certain discrepancy in consistency between its smooth surface and crimped edge. Thanks to this peculiarity, this sort of pasta is good with highly flavored sauces. It goes especially well with rich, lavish preparations.

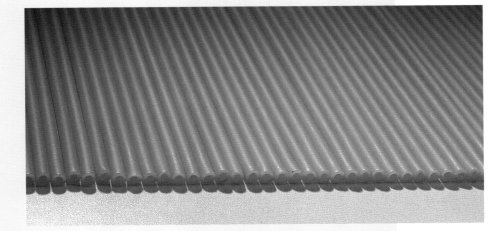

- MALTAGLIATI: literally, "badly cut" pasta.

- MEZZELUNE: crescent-shaped pasta.

- ORECCHIETTE: pasta in the shape of little ears, for thick, substantial sauces. Orecchiette comes from the ancient culinary tradition of Apulia, the region lying in the heel of southern Italy's "boot." These "little ears" (the meaning of "orecchiette") were once made individually by hand. You would cut off small strips from a skein of dough as thick as your thumb, and then shape them individually with your thumb on the pasta board. The inviting shape is good for all combinations, but especially for fish and vegetables.

- PAPPARDELLE: very broad ribbon pasta. These generous strips of pasta go best with hare and rabbit dishes served with thick sauces. Even the most demanding gourmets will be satisfied by creations such as these, with their full, powerful flavors. Pappardelle is said to have originated in central and northern Italy, and more specifically Tuscany, where it is still used in a considerable number of recipes.

- PASINE: A generic term for small pasta used in soups, such as *acini di pepe*, *ditali*, *risi*, and *stellini*.

■ PASTA ALL'UOVO: pasta with eggs.

■ PASTA INTEGRALE: whole-wheat pasta.

■ PENNE: cylinders of pasta cut diagonally. Penne owes its existence to the imagination of the Neapolitans and their love of good cooking. It is one of the most famous types of Italian pasta. Its diagonal cut gives the appearance of a quill, an ancient writing instrument (hence the name "penne," meaning "pen-quills"). The smooth, polished structure makes this pasta suitable for every type of sauce, though it goes particularly well with fresh, light ones.

■ PENNE LISCE: smooth penne for casseroles.

- PENNE RIGATE: fluted penne, used as classic vehicles for sauces. The deeply grooved surface seems designed to absorb different sauces, bringing out the flavor of thick, rich preparations as well as that of lighter sauces.

- PENNETTE: small penne with a short cooking time.

- PIZZOCCHERI: buckwheat pasta.

- RAVIOLI: rectangular pasta cases, filled with different ingredients; exquisite with butter-and-sage sauce and parmesan.

- RIGATONI: short, thick, fluted cylinders, good for dishes with plenty of sauce. Rigatoni comes from Rome and belongs to the tradition of typical Latin cookery. It is distinguished by a considerable diameter, plenty of space in the middle, and deep rills on the outside surface. The full, powerful structure is ideal for absorbing a sauce to the full extent of its inner and outer surface. This type of pasta will go well with any recipe, from the simplest to the most lavish and complicated dish.

- RISONI: pasta in the shape of grains of rice.

- ROTELLE/RUOTE: pasta twists.

- SEDANINI: small, gently curving tubes of pasta.

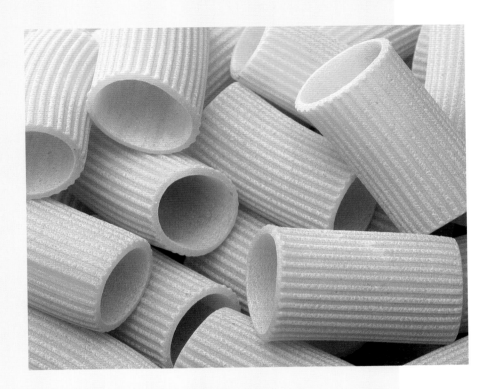

■ SPACCATELLE: short, curved pasta.

■ SPAGHETTI: long (sometimes very long), thin strands of pasta. Spaghetti comes originally from southern Italy and counts as the oldest, and also by far the most famous, of all types of pasta.

The origin of the name lies in the Italian word *spago*, referring to long, fairly thin threads of pasta dough, which after cooking curl up into fascinating coils on the plate. You cannot resist the game of entwining the spaghetti around your fork before tasting it!

These days, spaghetti is the symbol of Italian pasta and Mediterranean cookery. With its alluring shape, impeccable consistency in cooking, and many varied uses, spaghetti is the practical solution for countless imaginative recipes. It is a multi-faceted kind of pasta, going well with almost any sauce you can think of.

- SPAGHETTINI: very thin spaghetti with a short cooking time; goes very well with tomato sauce and more refined dishes.

- SPAGHETTONI: thick spaghetti.

- STELLINI: little stars.

- STRINGOLI: little rolls of short pasta.

- TAGLIATELLE: long ribbons of pasta twisted into nest-shapes, which are good for rich sauces. According to legend, a poetic and talented court cook drew his inspiration for tagliatelle from the hair of Lucrezia Borgia, and devoted this pasta to her on the occasion of her wedding to Alfonso d'Este. No other type of pasta can boast of such a romantic origin. Tagliatelle resembles fettuccine, which is slightly thinner, and is distinguished by the same versatility that makes it perfect for a range of fish, vegetable, and meat sauces.

- TAGLIATELLE VERDI: green-dyed ribbon pasta.

- TAGLIOLINI: very narrow ribbon pasta.

- TORTELLINI: ring-shaped pasta cases that can be filled with all sorts of ingredients—from vegetarian to meat or fish. Tortellini is also good for creamy sauces and goes well in clear soups.

- TORTELLONI: big, ring-shaped, filled pasta cases.

- TORTIGLIONI: short, ribbed, and twisted tubes of pasta that can effectively absorb the liquid of even very fine sauces. Used especially for rich sauces, but can also be broiled or baked in the oven.

- TRENETTE: corrugated ribbon pasta with a rough surface, ideal for dishes with plenty of sauce.

- TRINETTE: slender ribbon pasta with wavy edges.

- VERMICELLI: broad, flat spaghetti.

- VERMICELLINI: narrow, flat spaghetti.

- ZITI/ZITONI: short, thick macaroni.

Cooking and eating pasta

Cooking pasta

COOKING WITH ENJOYMENT

Cooking and serving pasta is something that can be done in any kitchen. You just put hot water in a saucepan, add the pasta, drain after a couple of minutes, and serve—it really is that quick! Of course, the better your kitchen equipment, the better your results will be—and the more you will enjoy the preparation.

PANS FOR PASTA

The size of the saucepan plays a decisive role. Generally speaking, the size of the pan is determined by the amount of pasta and type of pasta you wish to cook. As a rule, only big saucepans should be used, since for every 3½ oz (100g) of pasta you should use at least 32 oz (1 liter) of water. For long pasta varieties such as spaghetti, there are special cooking pans available. They are especially tall, so that every bit of the long pasta will come into contact with the hot water at the same time, and thus be evenly cooked.

Apart from this, there are of course pans that have been designed specifically for cooking pasta. These have an inside sieve, which enables the pasta to be taken directly out of the boiling water without straining it. These pans are commercially available under the general trade name of "pasta saucepans," though many of them are also marketed as asparagus pans.

Finally, pasta cooks can also buy models with a special lid, which covers the pan throughout the cooking time so that none of the heat is lost. The advantage of this method is that the temperature inside the pan remains constant.

SIEVES AND STRAINERS

It is recommendable to have a sufficiently big sieve or a strainer—if possible a metal one—for draining the pasta after cooking. The holes or mesh of the sieve should not be so big that they let small or thin pasta pieces slip through, but on the other hand not so small as to prevent the water from draining away quickly and thoroughly. The perfect sieve is as broad as they are high. Such types are to be recommended, not just when greater quantities of pasta are being cooked, but even for smaller amounts, as the freshly drained pasta can be shaken more easily in them so that the water efficiently drains away. Big sieves with two handles are especially practical to use, since you can grasp them firmly.

A good sieve will also have a stand, so that it can be placed securely in the sink or on the draining board. In this way, when pouring off the water you can hold the pasta pan with both hands.

SERVING POTS

Relatively new to the market are special pasta pots for quick cooking. These are designed so that the prepared pasta dishes can be served directly on the table, with impressive efficiency. Each pot has its own suitable sieve and tablemat, obviating the need to serve the pasta in an elaborate array of dishes and bowls. This also makes for less washing up.

Pasta al dente— the best way to cook it

Perfect pasta

Perfectly cooked pasta has the same status in *la cucina italiana* as a good cup of tea does in England. The most important thing is to find the right cooking time. In Italian cooking, this amounts to a small ceremony. Pasta should always be *al dente*. At this ideal point in the cooking process, the pasta is soft on the outside, but the inside—its heart—is still firm to the bite. Getting the timing right is fundamental to cooking pasta properly. Of course, so long as you heed a couple of basic rules, cooking perfect pasta is no real mystery.

1. USE PLENTY OF WATER: to cook pasta successfully, you need a large amount of water. This is crucial. As a rule of thumb:

FOR EVERY 3½ OZ (100 G) OF PASTA, USE 4 CUPS (1 LITER) OF WATER

Even more can be used if so desired. With too little water, the pasta sticks together. The water cannot wash around the individual pieces of pasta, which makes perfect pasta cooking impossible.

2. BRING THE WATER TO A BOIL: the pan should be exactly the right size for the burner on the stove—only in this way will you make the best use of the heat. The water should be bubbling vigorously.

QUICKER COOKING

The time needed to bring the water to a boil can be shortened with a high-power kettle. To begin with, simply bring a small amount of water to a boil in a pot, while at the same time heating the maximum amount of water in the kettle.

■ 3. SALT THE WATER: as soon as the water is bubbling, add salt. As a rule of thumb:

ADD 2 TSP (10 G) OF SALT FOR EVERY 4 CUPS (1 LITER) OF WATER

■ 4. ADD THE PASTA TO THE POT: as far as possible, add all the pasta at once to the pot, so that it will be uniformly cooked. Long pasta such as spaghetti should be allowed to slide slowly into the water.

LONG SPAGHETTI IN TOO-SMALL POTS

Especially where long spaghetti or spaghettini is concerned, you may find that you have no pots high or broad enough for the pasta to slip into the water all at the same time. In this case, first grasp the pasta in the middle with one hand and place it vertically over the pot.

Then, open your hand all at once, so that the pasta falls into the pot in a fan shape. This will stop the long pieces of pasta from sticking together. As soon as the water-covered pasta has softened a little, press down with a spoon or spatula onto the ends of the pasta, so that they are all pushed under the water. Then the pasta can be cooked as usual.

COOKING WITH OR WITHOUT OIL?

Does olive oil belong in the cooking water or not? This is a philosophical question among pasta lovers! Some are of the opinion that olive oil has no place in the water, since it would surround the pasta; as a result, later on, the pasta would be unable to absorb the sauce properly. Only in exceptional cases, e.g., with big pieces of pasta such as lasagna, or with fresh, thin pasta that would otherwise stick together, can a dash of oil be added to the cooking water. On the other hand, there are pasta devotees who think that olive oil in the cooking water is a must. Just the delicate aroma that the oil imparts to the water is something they cannot do without. And they prize the extra flavor the olive oil gives to the pasta. On one point the two factions are in agreement: if you cooked correctly, you do not need olive oil to prevent the pasta from sticking together.

5. COOKING: throughout the entire cooking time, the water should be gently bubbling in the pot. It is a good idea to stir the pasta around from time to time, so that it does not stick together or to the edges of the pot.

6. GETTING THE TIMING RIGHT: to get the right timing, taste individual pieces of pasta. The timing on the packet is just an indication. Real Italian cooks are reputed never to turn their backs on the pot while cooking pasta. The pasta is *al dente* when it is still firm to the bite yet soft enough to eat—i.e., it offers a certain resistance when you bite into it.

7. DRAINING THE PASTA: *pasta al dente* should then be immediately drained in a sieve. In no case should the cooked pasta be rinsed in cold water. Even rinsing it with hot water is a bad habit.

8. DO NOT ALLOW IT TO COOL: the pasta should on no account be allowed to cool. After draining, therefore, it should immediately be poured into a heated bowl.

9. MIX STRAIGHTAWAY: now that the pasta is ready, it is best to mix it immediately with the sauce. The still-porous surface of the freshly drained pasta will efficiently absorb the flavor of the sauce.

PRE-COOKING THE PASTA

Pasta that is to be further cooked after boiling, perhaps in a casserole, should be drained a little earlier, when still somewhat firmer. It will be cooked more thoroughly in the oven.

Serving pasta the right way

In simple, rustic manner or with style and elegance

If you look around at the choice of crockery on the market, you will find a wide selection of pasta plates and bowls. In addition, there is a vast range of accessories to accompany them, from olive bowls and breadbaskets to suitably "Italian" glasses.

So there are plenty of suggestions for serving pasta stylishly and elegantly. Center-stage are the big, deep pasta plates with their broad rims out of which, if you believe the ads, pasta can only *really* be enjoyed.

Anyone who takes a look at family tables as they are set in the actual motherland of pasta, however, will generally find neither special pasta plates nor expensive glasses. In Italy, spaghetti, tortellini, etc. are usually served quite simply.

Of course, there must be something for the eye to feed on too. In the final analysis, however, it is not the serving apparatus that determines how tasty a meal is, but the food itself. Big, deep pasta plates are to be recommended above all for dishes with runny sauces. Other pasta specialties can be served just as well—if not better—on flat plates. After all, however popular deep pasta plates may be, and however attractive they may look, you only ever look down on your meal from above—so the organization and artful arrangement of a dish can be admired more closely and effectively on a flat plate.

LOVINGLY ARRANGED TRIMMINGS

Meals that are light in color, i.e., with few color contrasts (such as béchamel sauce, filled pasta cases, or pasta carbonara), can be made to look more attractive with carefully chosen and arranged garnishes. Best of all are the classic ingredients of pasta cooking, such as fresh herbs, whole cherry tomatoes, or tomato slices, placed at the edge of the plate. But special additional ingredients (such as olives or spinach leaves) are also a suitable way of enhancing the appearance of a dish.

It is not just a nicely arranged plate that gives the table decoration a Mediterranean feel, however. It is the whole ensemble that creates the atmosphere: the tabletop or tablecloth, the little bowl of grated parmesan, the glasses for water and wine.

The basic rule is: the fuller the table, the more it contributes to the overall impression. Especially when seeking an authentic, somewhat more rustic ambience, you simply need to put on the table everything necessary for enjoying pasta. And when you also place a couple of summer flowers in a terracotta vase, the perfect "Italian atmosphere" is quickly achieved, even without any special pasta utensils.

THE RIGHT PORTIONS

The following portions per person are recommended (the figures refer to uncooked pasta):

- IN SOUP: 1–1½ oz (20–30 g)
- HORS D'OEUVRE: 2–2½ oz (50–60 g)
- SIDE DISH: 3–4 oz (80–100 g)
- MAIN COURSE: 4–6 oz (100–150 g)

Spaghetti tongs and spoons

When serving pasta, you need to distinguish between long, thin pasta on the one hand and short, thick pasta on the other. For long spaghetti, the best thing is to use serving tongs. These allow you to pick up the thin pasta most easily. A wide assortment can be found on the market, but the only real difference between them lies in their shape.

When purchasing tongs, it is a good idea to give them a quick tryout. You should test how easily the sides of the tongs can be pressed together and how securely the clasps close together. In addition, a great number of manufacturers produce spaghetti tongs that are designed to go with particular makes of flatware.

On the other hand, short, thick pasta is best served with a broad spoon. As a rule, big, salad flatware is equally suitable for serving pasta. Pasta is also easy to serve with a soup ladle, especially when the sauce is somewhat runny.

GRATED CHEESE AND PARMESAN BOWLS

There is no doubt about it: fresh pecorino or parmesan are as much part of the enjoyment of pasta as the sun is an essential part of summer. So hard cheese should always be available on the table when pasta is being served.

Even when the plates are filled in the kitchen and the pasta is served with ready-grated or sliced parmesan (or other cheese) on it, experience proves that many pasta connoisseurs like to sprinkle a little more on their meal.

There are two alternatives: either you can serve ready-grated hard cheese in a little bowl, or you can place a whole piece of cheese on the table, with a suitable grater. Both of these have their pros and cons. Serving the cheese in a little bowl is particularly suitable for a sophisticated ambience, when it would not really be right for individual guests to grate the cheese themselves. The disadvantage here is that you generally have some grated parmesan left over at the end of the meal. Having individual diners grate the cheese for themselves is, however, perfectly suitable when the pasta is being served in a more rustic setting. In addition, many pasta devotees obviously enjoy sprinkling the cheese freshly over the served meal themselves. The drawback here is that some parmesan almost always spills onto the table or table cloth.

Parmesan is best served on a large wooden board, on which the grater can also be set. A wide range of little hand graters is commercially available: these are the most suitable for an "Italian" table. In general, simple and economical models are perfectly adequate. For a finely grated hard cheese, there are special parmesan grinders. You should take special care when purchasing one of these, as the cheaper grinders can be very laborious to use.

SALT AND PEPPER

Finally, there should never be any lack of salt and pepper on a pasta table, since experience suggests that even pasta connoisseurs can find perfectly cooked (and properly salted) pasta too bland. Salt-shakers that finely grind the salt are to be recommended, as people can then add as much as they like, scattering the salt over their pasta in broad swathes.

Freshly ground pepper is a fundamental addition to many pasta dishes. The most stylish way of serving it is to grind the pepper over the meal once it has been served. In Italy, it is usual to use an over-sized pepper mill so that adding the pepper becomes something of a ceremony.

Pane—Bread

No pasta without bread

Pane (meaning "bread") is always served with meals in Italy. There is almost no meal that is not supplemented by bread (or bread-like cakes and pastries). It goes without saying, therefore, that bread is to pasta what salt is to soup.

Often, bread is not just a side dish, but fundamental to the meal, as in the case of the antipasti *bruschetta* and *crostini*. The Tuscan bread salad *panzanella*, made of slices of leftover bread soaked in water, is also well known.

Dishes such as this are often a sensible thing to serve, simply because most white bread is supposed to be eaten on the same day it is baked. In Italy, people almost exclusively eat white bread that has been made with yeast and corn. As a result, it soon dries up and loses its taste.

Flatbread (or pita)

Flatbread is the oldest kind of bread and originated across the regions as staple peasant fare. It is meant for immediate consumption, since it soon becomes brittle and hard. You do not need much to make it: flour, water, and perhaps a little salt. These ingredients are kneaded together, thinly rolled out, and baked on both sides on a hot surface made of cast iron, stone, or terracotta.

In addition, there are thicker types of flatbread made with yeast and baked in the oven. This type of bread, known as *focaccia*, is often baked with olive oil and coarse salt, or even with sardines, onions, olives, and cheese.

Loaves and rolls

Far more varied than flatbread in shape and size are the loaves and rolls made by Italian bakers. There is a wide range, from rustic peasant bread and fine pan loaves through plaited loaves, cracknels, and croissants. Specially shaped loaves are frequently prepared on special occasions. The type of bread that goes best with pasta is a little loaf made of pizza dough.

CIABATTA

Far and away the most famous Italian bread is ciabatta, a rustic type made from dough that has been stretched into a long, slender shape. The name means "slipper"—with the loaf often resembling a soft slipper. Ciabatta is baked from soft yeast dough with olive oil. It

is easy, but time-consuming, to prepare. Only after being allowed to rise several times does this popular bread gain its characteristic, soft, crumbly character, with big irregular pores and a thin, soft crust. Ciabatta is thus ideal for mopping up the remaining pasta sauce left on the plate.

Ciabatta dough, produced from wheat flour, water, yeast, sugar, olive oil and salt, can also be made into small loaves. These are called *ciabattini* and can usually be recognized from their almost square shape. Finally, just as famous as *ciabatta* is Tuscan white bread. It differs from other types of bread by being baked entirely without salt.

GRISSINI

Italian breadsticks or *grissini* are famous throughout the world. This specialty bread, made from white bread dough, is originally from Turin, but these days it is universally prized. Italians mostly serve grissini as antipasti, while in other places they are popular as a savory snack with wine or beer.

The right wine

NO PASTA WITHOUT WATER AND WINE

Water and wine—they are like brother and sister and belong equally and indispensably to the great community of the pasta table. Wine is made in every region of Italy, so it comes as no surprise that the juice of the vine is a fundamental accompaniment to pasta.

Which wine goes best with a particular pasta meal is open to endless debate, but there is one basic rule: it is stylish to serve a wine from the region in which the pasta dish originates. It does not always need to be red wine, even though more red than white wine is made and drunk in Italy itself. In the motherland of pasta, excellent white wines are also produced.

As with all wines, there are also considerable differences of quality in Italian wines. The time when Italy was mainly known as a source of cheap wine, however, is definitely past. The standard of Italian wine has risen considerably in the last few decades, and so even simple *vino da tavola* (table wine) can be recommended with pasta.

TEMPERATURE

At room temperature, chilled wine gets warmer at the rate of 3–4 °F (2 °C) per hour. So white wine is best served at the table in an ice bucket. Terracotta jars for keeping the wine chilled are very stylish.

Red wines are served at room temperature (about 72 °F/22 °C), while white wines are first chilled (to about 52–55 °F/11–13 °C). In addition, red wine and water are served in bigger glasses and white wine in smaller ones.

Important wines: an overview

Red wine:

- BARDOLINO: light and fresh, from the Veneto.

- BAROLO: a heavy wine from Piedmont.

- CHIANTI: dry and fruity, from Tuscany. *Chianti classico* comes from the region between Florence and Siena.

- DOLCETTO: mild, from Piedmont.

- LAMBRUSO: dry to sweet, from Emilia-Romagna.

- MONTEPULCIANO D'ABRUZZO: fruity, from Abruzzo.

White wine:

- FRASCATI: quaffable, from Latium.

- GALESTRO: light, from Tuscany.

- GAVI: elegant, from Piedmont.

- PINOT GRIGIO: tangy, from Friuli or the Trentino.

DETAILS FOUND ON WINE BOTTLES

On Italian wine bottles, you find the most varied designations and abbreviations. They are there to distinguish between the following types of wine:

- VINO CLASSICO: a wine from a particular (and specifically named) region of origin.
- VINO SCELTO: high-quality wine from selected grapes.
- VINO DOLCE: a very sweet wine.
- VINO AMABILE: a smooth wine.
- VINO SECCO: a dry wine.
- VINO SUPERIORE: a wine that has taken a long time to ripen.

The following abbreviations give you information about the wine's quality:

- DOC (*Denominazione di origine controllata*): wines from a particular vintage, whose production has been closely monitored. Not only the place of origin and the wine type, but also the quality of the grapes, the methods used in cultivation, harvesting, processing, and storage, as well as alcohol and acidity, are of prime importance for the classification.
- DOCG: wine that is evaluated according to even more searching criteria than DOC wine. DOCG wines are thus top-quality wines.
- IGT: wines from particular regions of a certain vintage.
- VDT (vino da tavola): table wine without indication of origin or vintage; the type of wine occupying the bottom rung of the quality scale.

Keeping and re-heating pasta

THE BEST WAY FOR KEEPING PASTA IN THE ICEBOX

Even in Italian cooking, it can happen that you sometimes cook a bit too much pasta and have some left over at the end of the meal. But pasta is, of course, very easy to keep. The following guidelines may be useful:

- In the icebox: 2 days
- In a * freezer compartment: 7 days
- In a ** freezer compartment: 3 weeks
- In a deep-freezer: 6 months

THE ART OF RE-HEATING CHILLED PASTA

Of course, connoisseurs will pull a face if you mention re-heating pasta. But it is certainly preferable to letting food go to waste. Re-heated pasta does not have to taste bad. Naturally, there are many opinions as to the best way of re-heating it. You can choose among the following methods:

- IN A SKILLET: put a little olive in a wide-based skillet and re-heat the pasta over low heat, stirring frequently. Butter can be used as an alternative to olive oil, if preferred.

- IN THE MICROWAVE: put the pasta in a microwavable container and heat, together with a small, microwavable bowl of water, on medium power.

- BY POURING HOT WATER OVER IT: with thin pasta, it is often enough to place it in a sieve and pour freshly boiled water over it. If the pasta is still not hot enough, stir and repeat the process.

- WITH STEAM: put the pasta in a sieve and hold this over a saucepan full of boiling water. Sieves with long handles that can be used to suspend it in the pan are the most suitable. Stir the pasta several times.

The most important ingredients for salsa and sugo

Richly endowed by nature

Italian cuisine is particularly rich. Innumerable ingredients can be used, from fish and meat and the most varied types of vegetables and herbs, to particular kinds of vinegar and oil. The rich variety of nature's bounty that is found under the Italian sun is fully reflected in pasta cookery.

Each individual region stresses different ingredients, and not everything you find in the saucepans of northern Italy will be used in the south—and vice versa.

All the same, there is a whole series of ingredients that play an important role in the preparation of pasta and pasta sauce, as well as the side dishes for pasta meals. The following pages list the most important ingredients, though trying to include the entire range for every pasta delicacy would go far beyond the limit of these pages.

Oil and Vinegar

OIL AND VINEGAR

There is hardly another ingredient that is so characteristic of pasta cookery as olive oil—so much so that we are completely justified in viewing it as the cornerstone of *la cucina italiana*.

The fundamental importance of olive oil should not however divert attention from the significance and quality of the second outstanding ingredient, *aceto balsamico*: that unique vinegar without which many classic meals would be unthinkable.

OLIVE OIL

Without olive oil, almost nothing in Italian cuisine—or indeed in the cookery of the entire Mediterranean region—would work. And since it is so popular, it is also called Italy's "liquid gold."

It has been known since ancient times that olive oil is good for the health. In contrast to animal fats like butter and vegetable fats such as margarine, olive oil is fundamentally healthier and more valuable.

SEVERAL KINDS

There are many kinds of olive oil. After the type and quality of the olives used, the taste and cost of an oil are mainly determined by the way the olives are pressed.

The Italians favor "extra virgin olive oil," which can be used both cooked and uncooked. Its advantage over other oils lies in the fact that it is produced exclusively through cold pressing and need not be subjected to any other treatment.

GUARANTEED QUALITY

The production of olive oil is carefully monitored in Italy. Especially good-quality oil is indicated by a protected designation of origin. These types of oil can be recognized from their trademark DOP (*Denominazione d'Origine Protetta*—protected label of origin) or IGP (*Indicazione geografica protetta*—protected geographical type).

The granting of a label of origin is meant to protect the typical qualities of the region from which an extra virgin olive oil comes.

Among the best-known protected types of olive oil are: Brisighella, Colli del Trasimeno, Apruntino Pescarese, and Val di Mazara. Olive oil of the highest quality is also produced in numerous other regions of Italy: Liguria in the north, Tuscany, Apulia, and Lucania in the south.

Different types of olive oil have very different properties, depending on their place of origin. The basic characteristics of an oil vary from one region to another: the color range extends from straw yellow to green, and the taste is reminis-

TESTING OLIVE OIL CORRECTLY

The taste of olive oil is best tested with a piece of white bread that has as neutral a flavor as possible (thus you should not use, for example, a bruschetta that has been baked with olive oil). Allow a little oil to trickle onto a small plate and then soak the bread in it. Anyone testing different types of olive oil should take a sip of water (still, not sparkling) in between.

ORGANIC OLIVE OIL

For some time now, organic olive oil has also been available on the market. This type comes from olive groves that are treated neither with chemical fertilizer nor with pesticides.

cent not just of fresh olives, but is frequently also fruity or similar to certain vegetables in flavor. The taste, finally, can be more or less distinctive.

ACETO BALSAMICO

This famous balsamic vinegar is fundamental to Italian cookery. It is exclusively produced in the province of Modena, in accordance with a procedure that has remained unchanged for hundreds of years, using special *acetaia* or vinegar barrels.

The best quality *aceto balsamico* is produced if possible from local wine grapes, in particular Lambrusco and Trebbiano. The grapes ripen as fermented must in the little barrels that are characteristic of *aceto balsamico*. Then it is a matter of pressing the must, which is then boiled until it has been reduced to half its volume. After that, it is poured into the *batterie*—this word

designates a series of little barrels made of oak, mulberry, chestnut, or cherry-tree wood, in which the acetic acid is cooked and stored for several decades. Each year, the vinegar is transferred into another barrel. This is a real ritual: the vinegar meant for consumption is tapped off from the smallest barrel in the *batterie*, and the biggest barrel is refilled with fermented must. The rest is a matter of time, but also depends on the patience of the vinegar producer, who keeps a close eye on the proceedings in the *acetaia*.

Long storage ensures quality

Many factors are responsible for the quality of balsamic vinegar, but ageing plays the most important role. Twelve years are enough for "young" balsamic vinegar, which will already taste very good on the palate. The difference, however, between this and 25- or 50-year-old balsamic vinegar is clearly perceptible—the taste continually improves.

Vegetables

THE BOUNTY OF NATURE

Italian kitchens have at their disposal an incredible range of vegetables that can be used both as independent dishes and as the basic ingredients for a wide variety of pasta sauces.

Favored by nature, the climate and the soil, every type of vegetable flourishes from northern Italy through the fertile fields of central Italy, to the southernmost tip of Sicily: artichokes, beans, peas, asparagus, cabbage, pumpkins, zucchini, paprika, eggplant, fennel, boletus mushrooms and truffles.

Italian vegetable dishes are world-famous—not only because of their simplicity, but above all because only fresh market produce is considered acceptable for cooking.

The favorite, though actually of course a fruit, is the tomato. Nothing else is so closely linked with the way we think of Italian cookery. The boletus mushroom, however, which is a special and exclusively typical Italian ingredient, is also frequently used in the most varied pasta recipes, as is zucchini, which is especially good for you and goes very well with pasta.

Pomodori: tomatoes

Tomatoes are juicy, red, malaceous fruits of Central American origin. In Italian they are called *pomodori*, which means "golden apples." They are cultivated throughout Italy, predominantly in the south, but also throughout the Po valley.

Real connoisseurs agree that every recipe should be prepared using the right kind of tomato. And thanks to technical progress in cultivation, it is possible these days to buy fresh tomatoes in every season.

The most widespread types of tomato are San Marzano and Pachino, but there are also cherry tomatoes and ribbed tomatoes.

SKINNING TOMATOES

Tomatoes are always found on the list of ingredients for salsa or sugo, but before they are actually cooked in these sauces they need to be skinned. All you need is a sharp knife and boiling water.

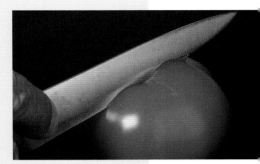

While the water is being brought to a boil, free the tomatoes from their green stem and then cut a 1 in (0.5 cm)-deep cross into them at the top. Then put the tomatoes into the boiling water for a minute, to blanch them. The easiest thing to do is to lower them in with a ladle.

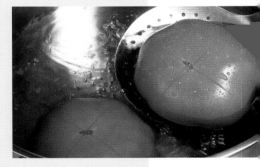

CUORI DI BUE

Browned tomatoes, the so-called *cuori di bue*, meaning, "ox hearts", are an Italian specialty. To make them, first cut the tomatoes breadthways and remove some of the flesh. Mix the flesh with breadcrumbs, parsley, and garlic, fill the tomato with the mixture, and allow it to brown in the oven in an ovenproof dish at a temperature of 350–400°F (180–200 °C).

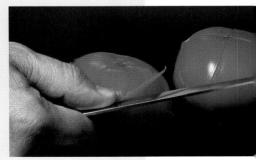

After giving them a hot bath, you briefly let the tomatoes cool. Then you remove the skins with a knife, starting from the cross cut into the tomato and pulling the flap downwards.

How long the tomatoes remain in the hot water is a decisive point. If you dip them in for too short a time, the skin will not come away from the flesh of the tomato. If you leave them in the water too long, the inside of the tomato gets too soft and squashy for the skin to be cleanly pulled away. The seeds are usually removed before continuing with the recipe.

SAN MARZANO

The Italian type of tomato known as "San Marzano," with its characteristic bottle shape, is well suited to tomato sauces of

every kind. In its motherland, this kind of tomato is not just used in cooking: San Marzano tomatoes can also be eaten in salads or on a classic bruschetta. In this case, the tomatoes are cut into small cubes and served with garlic and a few drops of olive oil on a slice of toasted bread.

Next to the San Marzano tomato, the "Ventura" variety is the sort most frequently cooked in Italy. Both types are particularly well suited to make *pomodori pelati*, i.e., canned tomatoes that can be used to cook pasta sauces at any time, instead of fresh, skinned tomatoes.

By stirring tomato purée into the sauce, you can achieve a very intense tomato flavor. But be careful: there is an art to "spicing up" a sauce with tomato purée. The basic rule for beginners is: start with a small quantity, taste, and then if necessary add a little more.

TIDBITS

Cherry or *pachino* tomatoes are cultivated in central and southern Italy. They do not simply taste delicious, but are also excellent as a garnish. Try them with pasta, oil, a salted anchovy, or zucchini. In every combination, these tiny tomatoes create an intensely flavorsome mixture of southern tastes.

BOLETUS MUSHROOMS

DRIED BOLETUS MUSHROOMS

Outside the mushroom season, you can obtain dried boletus mushrooms in jars. These preserved mushrooms are hardly any less tasty than the fresh ones. Dried mushrooms should be soaked for 1–2 hours before cooking.

The undisputed king of mushrooms in an Italian kitchen is the boletus mushroom, distinguished by its pleasant consistency and wonderful flavor. With its characteristic round crown that becomes slippery in the rain and then tends to get hard and cracked, it looks like everyone's idea of a typical mushroom. In addition, boletus mushrooms grow in every region of Italy, in particular in cultivated woods with tall trees.

"Boletus mushroom" is a generic term, with several different species belonging to the kind. The best-known type is *boletus edulis*, which can be collected in basketfuls in the fall, but we should not forget the *boletus aestivalis*, which is usually around from the start of the season, sometimes even in May. Lovers of the woods have given this mushroom several other names, from region to region—*brisa*, for instance, and *cuzzolotto* are just two of the many different terms that are found in the vocabulary of mushroom gatherers.

Next to boletus mushrooms, brown and white mushrooms should figure in our account of pasta cooking. Their great advantage is that they are less expensive. Apart from these, Italians also cook with every other common kind of mushroom, such as chanterelles or morels.

All mushrooms need to be cleaned before cooking, ideally through careful brushing. You can also rub them down with a very lightly dampened cloth. On no account, however, should the mushrooms be washed in water. Once they have been cleaned, the stems should be scraped with a small knife.

BOLETUS MUSHROOMS AS ANTIPASTI

Uncooked boletus mushrooms are popular antipasti in Italy. Carefully remove the crown from the stem and cut it into thin slices. Arrange these fanwise on a plate and drizzle with olive oil. Then add a pinch of pepper and a few slices of mature parmigiano reggiano, and serve cold.

ZUCCHINI

Zucchini is the fruit of a Central American pumpkin plant that flourishes best in a moderately warm climate with a great deal of sun and not much wind. Thus zucchini finds in several regions of Italy the ideal terrain for growth. In the whole of Italy, several different sorts of zucchini are cultivated: the *striata d'Italia* with its long shape and characteristic stripes; the *verde di Milano* with its firm flesh; the *faentina* with its cudgel shape and bright coloration; and the *rigata pugliese*, *veneziana*, and *bianca sarda*.

Italian varieties of zucchini can be served fresh from late spring to summer. At all other times of the year, imported zucchini is of course widely available.

In the spring, you commonly find zucchini on the market that still has its yellow blossoms. These can be used very effectively for stuffing, or else deep-fried.

Preparing zucchini for cooking is not particularly labor-intensive. You simply need to give it a good wash, and free it from its stems and blossoms. Of course, the latter is not necessary if you are going to stuff the zucchini.

Then there are all sorts of ways to prepare it although it is in fact quite enough just to brown the chopped zucchini briefly in a little olive oil with salt and pepper. The pasta (whether spaghetti or *tortellini*) will then taste simply wonderful.

Zucchini is extremely good for you. It is exceptionally low in calories (14 calories per 100 g) and high in potassium content (200 mg per 100 g). In addition, it is an important source of vitamins. In particular, it contains vitamins K and C.

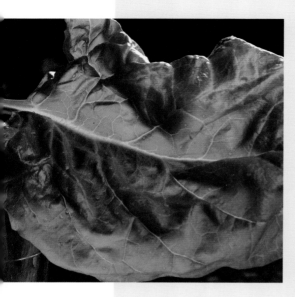

SPINACH

Spinach belongs to the family of goosefoot plants (botanical name Chenopodiaceae), and is also very popular in Italian cooking: in oven-cooked puddings (as well as for lasagna or cannelloni) it enjoys high esteem, and is also frequently used for filling various kinds of pasta or to dye the pasta dough.

Fresh spinach is either served with or without its roots (in the latter case it is known as "leaf spinach.") It is available all year round: in spring and summer it is delicate, in winter somewhat coarser. Spring and summer spinach has very tender leaves that are good, uncooked, in salads. Autumn and winter spinach, with its strong and often slightly wavy leaves, is more suitable for blanching.

NEVER RE-HEAT

Spinach should only ever be cooked once and never re-heated, since otherwise it can release harmful nitrite.

When tossed in butter, shallots, and garlic, fresh spinach is a real delicacy. Uncooked, puréed spinach also makes an excellent dye for homemade pasta.

As well as being a tasty ingredient in cooking, spinach is also a vegetable with a high mineral and vitamin content. Unfortunately, it also comes with high levels of nitrates and oxalic acid.

Fresh, young spinach should be carefully selected and thoroughly washed in plenty of cold water before being consumed.

CAPERS

Capers are the flower buds of the caper bush that grows wild or is cultivated in many regions of South Italy. Especially tasty capers come from the Lipari (or Aeolian) islands north of Sicily, and from the island of Pantelleria west of Sicily.

ADD AT THE END

Capers should only ever be added to a dish just before the end of the cooking time. If you cook them any longer, they lose their flavor.

In ancient times, capers were prized not just for their gastronomic advantages, but also for their medicinal value, due to their diuretic, digestive, and even aphrodisiac properties. After harvesting (which is still done by hand), the capers are treated with sea-salt for a few days. Only after this process has rid them of their extremely bitter taste are the capers finally pickled in salt or brine for preservation.

Because of this method of preservation, it is best to rinse the capers carefully before using them in cooking. Meals with capers need to be salted only sparingly.

Capers go very well with tomatoes and olives. Pasta or main courses that might otherwise seem rather colorless gain extra zest from capers.

Combining them with anchovies is demonstrative proof that, even in Mediterranean cookery, brevity is the soul of wit. Even before the pasta water has reached boiling point, this simple but exquisite recipe is practically done. Place the anchovies in a pan with olive oil and add a clove of garlic and a few capers. Then stir until the anchovies form a cream. Before serving, briefly cook the pasta *al dente* (*fusilli* is ideal for the purpose) in the sauce.

GARLIC AND ONIONS

Allium sativum is the Latin name for garlic, which belongs to the same family as leeks and is thus a close relative of onions, shallots, chives, and, of course, leeks. Together with onions, it is an irreplaceable ingredient in many Italian dishes.

Garlic is a plant that grows to about 28 in (70 cm); it consists of a nodule with a tubular stem and long, thin leaves. The nodule is formed from an egg-shaped main bulb and some 12 or so secondary bulbs called "cloves."

In the kitchen, garlic is a universal herb for every kind of piquant dish. The undisputed classic among pasta dishes is

doubtless spaghetti with garlic, oil, and peperoncini, the so-called *spaghetti aglio, olio e peperoncini* (see p. 136).

Garlic also increases the savor of many main courses. All you need to do is put garlic and basil in the blender for a few moments to obtain an excellent mix of herbs that can be used, for instance, to toss a juicy piece of meat in the pan. The flavor of oil and vinegar too can be greatly improved by adding garlic. Chop up a few cloves of garlic and leave them to soak in the vinegar or oil for a few weeks.

In Italy, however, garlic is also prepared *in camicia* (literally, "in its shirt.") The cloves are cooked or sautéed whole, with their skins still on, so as to avoid an over-powerful taste. You obtain the fullest aroma when you use fresh garlic.

In cooking, you generally squeeze the peeled garlic cloves in a small garlic press. You can, however, do it much more simply. The quickest way is to cut the peeled garlic into thin slices and then sprinkle these with salt. The salt softens up the structure of the garlic within a few minutes. Then you can simply squeeze the garlic slices with the back of a knife. This "garlic paste" can very easily be stirred into sauces in whatever proportion you want. Of course, you must then make sure that you do not add too much more salt, since the salt in the garlic remains in the dish.

One practical way of using garlic in cooking is to use the powdered form. This has the added advantage of preserving its flavor for longer, as long as the container is kept in a cool, dark place.

In some circumstances, garlic can be difficult to digest. The allicin contained in the fragrant cloves is responsible for this. Removing the central green shoot from the cloves generally solves the problem.

OLIVES

Olives are fundamental to Italian cookery—and not just in the shape of olive oil, without which Mediterranean cuisine is unthinkable. Olives themselves are a tasty ingredient in countless dishes.

The taste varies essentially from one type or "cultivar"—as olive specialists refer to them—to another. One well-known type, for example, is *bella di cerignola*, from which several Apulian olive oils are produced. The select type *nocellara del bellice* is highly prized in Italy, as are olives from Taggia, which are distinguished by their very mild taste and crunchy flesh.

A complete list of olives would need to contain at least another 700 cultivars—proof of the thousands of years of history behind the cultivation of this plant in Italy. The olive tree on which the olive fruit grows is very sensitive to cold. A healthy plant can be killed off by a single frost. In addition to this, there is

a pest called the olive fly that can cause considerable damage to the plants, thus forcing growers to use pesticides.

Olive picking is done by hand. The branches are shaken with long poles, though special machines can also be used to shake the olives down from the tree.

In the kitchen, olives are frequently to be found in the preparation of tasty sauces: for instance, in a classic tuna fish sauce with olives that goes very well with *pipe rigate*. Another typical meal in the Mediterranean tradition is *bavettine* with capers, olives, and anchovies. A special type of dish in central Italy is Ascolano olives—pitted olives stuffed with meat, wrapped in dough, coated with breadcrumbs, deep-fried, and served hot.

A LONG HISTORY

The olive tree has been part of Mediterranean culture since time immemorial. The Greeks dedicated it to Athena and the Romans to Minerva, with its branches being used (as were laurels) to crown the heads of victorious generals.

Herbs and Spices

GUARANTEEING TASTE

Herbs are always used in Italian cooking, and are usually fresh. In the Italian kitchen you will generally find, as absolute essentials, rosemary, basil, sage, oregano, and parsley. But if you do not have fresh herbs, you can of course use dried ones. Do not forget, however, when measuring out the quantities, that these have a more intense taste than fresh herbs. Leftover fresh herbs can be frozen in small portions, but should be washed and, if necessary, chopped beforehand.

BASIL

Of all the herbs that impart a particular flavor to sauces and dishes, basil plays a particular role. Its name comes from the Greek word *basilikon*, meaning "kingly"—and it does indeed have a corresponding significance in *la cucina italiana*. Basil is highly prized throughout Italy. In Liguria, there is even a special association devoted to basil, with the aim of fostering its use in local gastronomy. And in Diano Marina, in Liguria, basil has its own, popular festival.

The homeland of basil is the Indian subcontinent, but by Roman times it was already being cultivated in Italy. Basil is an annual, with big, vivid green, oval leaves. The stronger the sunlight on the plants, the more intense is their flavor. Basil tastes sweet and spicy, with a pleasantly peppery tang. So it can really liven up a meal. The leaves can be used both fresh and dried; the latter have a slightly piquant flavor.

In herbal medicine and chemistry, a variety of attempts have been made to unlock the mysterious nature of basil and the secrets of its highly individual flavor. It was discovered that at least 20 flavor components make up its aroma: combined in different proportions, they alter its taste. So every sort has its own characteristic flavor—sometimes resembling lemon, sometimes mint.

Its green color can also be used to replace spinach in the dyeing of pasta. For every 2½ lb (1 kilo) of flour, 4 oz (100 g) purified basil leaves have to be worked into the dough. Basil plants can be obtained commercially anywhere, and you can easily grow them yourself during the spring and summer in a window box or in the garden. You can freeze the leaves and store them, so that even in the cold winter months you will have enough for use in your kitchen.

OREGANO

Oregano is the classic spice of Italian cooking. You can hardly imagine Italian meals without this bushy, leafy herb, whether you are cooking pasta or pizza, or fruity, tangy sauces. Oregano is the main ingredient in any Italian mix of herbs, which will also include paprika, pepper, thyme, and sometimes also salt and chili.

Oregano has a spicy, bitter taste, but (when fresh) quite a pleasant one. It has a very intense odor and belongs to the Mediterranean area. Its flavor grows more intense the longer it is left out in the sunlight.

According to legend, oregano was created by the Greek goddess Aphrodite, as a symbol of joy—thus newlyweds were crowned with oregano. The herb was also considered to be a surefire way of preventing the groom's affections from straying.

The odor and taste of oregano depend on the essential oils carvacrol and thymol, and are similar to those of marjoram. Marjoram and oregano are indeed related species. So oregano is often called "wild marjoram," though the two herbs do not actually go very well together in cooking.

Oregano leaves can be used fresh or dried. Fresh oregano should be wrapped up in damp paper towels as quickly as possible, and kept in a freezer bag in the vegetable compartment of the icebox. This way, you can keep it for three to four days.

The flavor of dried oregano is more intense than that of fresh oregano. It comes out best when cooked for just a short time.

PARSLEY

The Italian type of parsley is not crinkly, but smooth. The Mediterranean variety has a more intense flavor than other kinds (such as German parsley) and is often added as an ingredient to bring out the taste of the cooking. Despite this, it is so mild in taste that it can be worked into the meal in great quantities. Since the stems have a more delicate flavor, the leaves can be replaced by the stems in dishes that would be swamped by an over-intense flavor.

ROSEMARY

Rosemary was already a sacred herb in antiquity. It was dedicated to the goddess Aphrodite and was viewed as a fertility symbol, but it was also generally considered as a symbol of fidelity and reliability—and consuming it was supposed to strengthen the memory.

These days, rosemary is counted as one of the classic herbs of Italian cuisine. Its leaves are often used to spice up game, lamb, poultry, and pork. But it also goes extremely well with fruity vegetables such as tomatoes, zucchini, and eggplants.

Rosemary is native to the whole Mediterranean region, where it still grows wild. It is a small, evergreen shrub that cannot tolerate frost. In shape, its leaves are somewhat reminiscent of pine needles. Rosemary loves the sunshine and does not thrive in wet conditions—it is a real southerner.

Rosemary has a resinous, spicy taste and, when fresh, has a pungent smell. When dried, it should be used only sparingly, since otherwise it can taste bitter. Rosemary should be added near the start of cooking, and its sprigs removed before serving.

One thing to remember is that fresh rosemary sprigs are exceptionally good as skewers for meat or vegetable. They look attractive, while flavoring the food at the same time.

Rosemary, like other typically Italian herbs, can be purchased in practically any large supermarket.

Rosemary is also used for medicinal purposes: it helps to relieve fatigue, and has a soothing effect on the nervous and circulatory systems. It is also sometimes employed against stomachache and headache. As a salve, rosemary helps treat rheumatism, neuritis, and cramp.

SAGE

Tortellini with sage butter, *saltimbocca* and polenta with gorgonzola and sage—these are absolute classics of *la cucina italiana*.

SEA-DEW: AN ALMOST LATIN NAME

The word "rosemary" is made up of the two Latin words *ros* and *marinus*, meaning "dew" and "sea" respectively. Hence rosemary is sometimes called "sea-dew."

Their typical taste is brought out especially by the use of the roots of the sage plant—and sage is one of the traditional Italian herbs. It is recognized by its oval and slightly hairy leaves, and is rich in essential oils, especially thujane. The leaves have a highly aromatic smell and taste fresh, tangy, and slightly bitter.

Too much of this fine herb can create a soapy taste, so it should be used only sparingly, as its flavor can easily swamp others. It develops a particularly full taste when fried directly in fat.

Together with sage's use in the kitchen (where it is not just suitable for pasta, but also very effective with tomatoes and potatoes as well as minced meat and stuffing for poultry), it is also famous for its medicinal properties. One need only think of the various cough drops that people suck when they have sore throats—these are often made from sage.

THYME

Thyme in its many varieties is a further basic constituent of pasta cookery. Several types have gray-green leaves and a pungent flavor, while others have dark green leaves and a more volatile flavor. The smell of thyme is just as important as its taste. Its essential oils play an important role in this, especially thymol and carvacrol. The odor is always very intense. While, for instance, wild thyme has a powerfully tangy and bitter smell, lemon thyme gives off a delicate, lemon odor when heated.

Thyme goes outstandingly well with fruity sauces and soups, but also with salads, meat and cabbage dishes, and fish terrines. Zucchini, eggplants, and tomatoes are often flavored with thyme. Just a small quantity of this herb is generally required, and it can be cooked for quite a long time without any problem.

Peperoncini

Small red and green chilies, called *peperoncini* in Italian, are particularly prized in southern Italy, and used to spice up almost every kind of meal—though the pods can be painfully hot.

Peperoncini were brought to Europe only after the discovery of the New World. In Italy they have been cultivated only since the 19th century. Ever since, they have been a valued part of Italian cuisine.

In Italy, a distinction is drawn between the larger *peperoni*, bell peppers, and the smaller *peperoncini* that are used as spices.

MAKING IT MILDER

If you want to reduce somewhat the hot, spicy flavor of the little pods, you should carefully remove seeds and ribs.

The latter are especially popular in Calabria, where restaurant tables are often set with dried chilies next to the salt and pepper, so that people can flavor their meals as they wish. And in Calabria there is not just an annual *peperoncini* festival, but even a museum devoted entirely to this piquant plant.

Peperoncini can give even simple dishes (such as a plate of pasta with garlic and olive oil) an extra dash of flavor, and impart a long-lasting, distinctive taste to any meal.

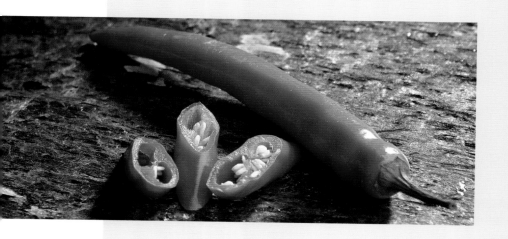

PINE NUTS

Pine nuts (also known as pignolia) ripen in the cones of pine trees (also known as umbrella pines). The kernels have to be removed from the cones by hand, so they can be costly. Pine nuts are popular in Italian cooking and a permanent fixture in many pasta sauces—one need only think of the famous *pesto alla genovese* (see p. 194). Other dishes in *la cucina italiana* are also given an extra dash of flavor by these little, golden-yellow kernels. Thus in Genoa, fish is often served with a *salsa di pinoli*; in Sicily, the kernels are used for piquant fillings with rice and raisins; and throughout Italy, they are used to flavor sweet dishes.

The kernels have a sweetish, resinous flavor and are very good for you: they contain the minerals calcium, iron, and phosphorus as well as vitamins of the B-group and vitamin A.

Since pine nuts have a relatively high fat content, they easily turn rancid. So they are best bought in small quantities and kept in a cool place, and above all not stored for too long before use.

Additional ingredients

STAYING FAITHFUL TO THE ORIGINS

Fennel and mangold wurzels, potatoes and carrots, peas and beans: despite the importance of tomatoes, basil, etc., there are countless other vegetables that can be used in pasta cooking.

Originally, the regions in which these ingredients were cultivated played a decisive role. Certain dishes were found only in the areas where particular types of vegetable were grown. These days, however, people cook with every possible ingredient in all parts of Italy, with regional specialties becoming universally successful while continuing to enjoy considerable popularity in their places of origin.

Unlike in other European countries, however, people have generally remained faithful to the indigenous fruits of nature that flourish from north to south in Italy. You will not, as a rule, find anything exotic in *la cucina italiana*. But Italians also cook with an ingredient that is rarely found in the recipes of other countries: anchovies.

Anchovies

It is difficult to imagine Italian cookery without anchovies. They function first and foremost as a way of spicing up a meal. Indeed, they are deliberately included in the most varied of recipes. Especially in southern Italy and Sicily, there is a series of traditional dishes that cannot do without anchovies. But in central and northern Italy too, these little fish have been prized for centuries as an ingredient in pasta dishes.

Once they have been caught, anchovies are generally pickled in salt or oil, and are commercially available under the name *acciughe*. They are often flavored with spicy sauces.

As a rule, the fleshier the anchovies, the more intense and rounded their flavor. Especially rich in taste are the anchovies pickled in salt: these can be bought individually, out of big cans, or else by weight. Salted anchovies should always be washed thoroughly in running water before they are used. This considerably lessens the salt content. Even when the

Buying the right type of anchovy

If you are cooking from a recipe, you should take special care when anchovies are part of it. It makes a big difference to the taste whether you buy seasoned anchovies (i.e., in cans or as anchovy paste in tubes), or whether you go for pickled anchovies that come without additives, flavorings, and seasonings.

anchovies have been given a good rinsing, it is important to be careful when salting the pasta dish, tasting it to guard against over-salting. Using anchovy fillets pickled in oil reduces the problem.

To improve the quality of the sauces, you can obtain ready-made anchovy paste in tubes. This is a paste made of anchovies, salt, and a little vinegar, the taste of which has been improved by the addition of various herbs.

Cheese

PASTA: ATTENTION TO EVERY LAST LITTLE DETAIL

"The French cook with water—and wine!" This was how the star chef Paul Bocuse once described the secret of French cuisine. Likewise, we might say that the formula for Italian cuisine goes: "The Italians cook their pasta with water—and cheese!" For there is hardly any meal in Italy that does not feature cheese.

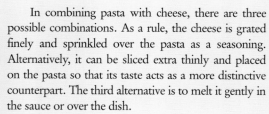

In combining pasta with cheese, there are three possible combinations. As a rule, the cheese is grated finely and sprinkled over the pasta as a seasoning. Alternatively, it can be sliced extra thinly and placed on the pasta so that its taste acts as a more distinctive counterpart. The third alternative is to melt it gently in the sauce or over the dish.

In Italian cookery, it is not just the famous *grana* (hard cheese) that is used. No less important are slicing cheeses, blue vein cheeses, and cream cheeses.

How to buy and use cheese

Hard cheese is best bought by the piece. You should grate it only when you are about to use it, so that it always tastes fresh and flavorsome.

You can keep cheese by wrapping it carefully in waxed paper or perforated aluminum foil. Hard cheese can be kept in the vegetable compartment of the icebox for up to two months. Different varieties of cheese should be wrapped separately, of course. Soft cheeses can easily be frozen. But hard cheese is not suitable for freezing, since it becomes crumbly.

HARD CHEESE

Hard cheese, called *grana* (meaning "grain") in Italian, is especially good for grating, thanks to its texture. Hence it provides good seasoning. A well-ripened, perfect *grana* cheese has a slightly granular structure and is easier to break into pieces than cut with a knife. The surface of the break then shows the cheese's typical flaky structure.

There is a very wide selection of hard cheeses in Italy, but on an international level you can also find a good selection in well-stocked specialty shops. The best-known and most important types of *grana* cheese include:

■ PARMIGIANO REGGIANO: this *grana* is also known as "parmesan," for short. It is, of course, the best known and doubtless also the most typical Italian cheese for pasta. It is a half-fat (32 percent fat dry weight) and extra-hard cheese made of cows' milk and takes at least one year, but usually two to three, to ripen. *Parmigiano reggiano* is distinguished by its spicy, piquant, but never sharp taste. It comes from Emilia-Romagna.

When young, it is eaten as a table cheese; when old, it is used in cooking and for grating. But even when sliced very thinly it can brighten up salads or *carpaccio*. It is often used together with mild mozzarella or other, less intense, types of cheese. In Italy it is also served in small, crumbly pieces as an appetizer.

Parmigiano reggiano is found shrink-wrapped in most well-stocked supermarkets as well as in "country" delicatessens that offer a good selection of cheeses.

■ GRANA PADANO: this cheese is very similar to parmesan, and is equally good for grating. *Grana padano* is produced from cow's milk and is mild, slightly acidic, and savory in taste. It has a fat content of 32 percent dry weight.

When it has not yet fully ripened, *grana padano* can also be used effectively as a slicing cheese; later on, it is only good for grating. This kind of cheese comes from Emilia-Romagna, too, but it is also produced in Lombardy and Piedmont. *Grana padano* can also be

found shrink-wrapped at the supermarket or in specialty cheese stores. Internationally, it is often passed off as parmesan, but as a rule it is cheaper than *parmigiano reggiano*, being produced in much greater quantities.

■ PECORINO: this cheese, which is produced exclusively from fresh ewe's milk, claims to be one of the oldest sorts in the world. It is said to have already been a delicacy among the ancient Romans. *Pecorino* is slightly salty and piquant, with a somewhat sharp, intense odor. The grating variety is ripened for longer, and is stronger, but not too intense, in taste. If it comes from Latium or Sardinia, it is called *pecorino romano*; if it comes from Sicily, *pecorino siciliano*. Its fat content is 36 percent dry weight.

When young, *pecorino* is enjoyed with *ciabatta* or in wafer-thin slices as a snack. It is sprinkled in grated form over soups and pasta dishes. *Pecorino romano* is not so easy to come by, but you can obtain it in specialty cheese or Italian stores.

MOTASIO: this tasty hard cheese comes from Friuli and the Veneto. Its flavor becomes even more pronounced as it ripens. *Motasio* is also produced from cow's milk. Its fat content is 40 percent dry weight.

When young, *motasio* is eaten with bread; when ripened, it is mainly used for broiling.

This sort of cheese is mostly found, outside Italy, only in well-stocked specialty cheese or Italian stores.

■ CACIOCAVALLO: this full-fat *filata* cheese made of cow's milk is produced throughout southern Italy. It is famous for its odd pear-shape—it is sometimes even called "pear-shaped cheese." *Caciocavallo* is flavorsome, melts in the mouth, and is generally delicate and predominantly mild in taste.

A young *caciocavallo* can be enjoyed with bread or as an antipasto. The older it gets, the less suitable it is to be eaten uncooked. It is then used mainly for grating. Its fat content is 38 percent dry weight.

■ PROVOLONE: When young it has a mild and sweetish taste, when somewhat older it resembles butter, and when fully ripened it has a strong, piquant taste. Because of its excellent qualities when melted, it is highly suitable for broiling on top of casseroles and pasta dishes. Its fat content is 44 percent dry weight.

SLICING CHEESES

■ ASAGIO: this half-fat, cow's milk slicing cheese (20 percent or more fat dry weight) comes from the Veneto and Friuli. It has a pleasantly spicy taste, nutty and with a slight after-taste of lemon. Mature *asagio* goes very well with *ciabatta*. An old *asagio* is best used for grating.

■ BEL PAESE: the name means "beautiful country," and it was created in Milan at the beginning of the 18th century, as a creamy butter cheese with a delicate yellow color. It has a mild, tart flavor.

- FONTINA: this cheese from Val d'Aosta is a mild and flavorsome, full-fat table cheese (45 percent fat dry weight). It melts easily and is therefore especially good for broiling and for fondue recipes such as *fonduta*, the Piedmont variant of the Swiss cheese fondue.

- TALEGGIO: this full-fat, cow's milk slicing cheese is distinguished by its very subtle, spicy flavor—intense, nutty, and fresh. It has an odor that is discreetly reminiscent of cow. *Taleggio* has a fat content of 48 percent fat dry weight and is served as a table cheese. It comes originally from the plain of the same name near Bergamo, though these days it is also produced in other regions of Italy.

Taleggio with fruit and walnut bread is the ideal conclusion to an Italian meal. Because it melts very easily, it is often stirred into various dishes.

Cream cheese

- MOZZARELLA: this full-fat cheese, from Campania and Latium, is one of the most renowned specialty cheeses of Italy. So it comes as no surprise to learn that it is now produced throughout Italy. Traditionally, buffalo's milk is used in the production of mozzarella. These days, however, it is mostly made from cow's milk.

Mozzarella has a mild, sour taste, ranging from milky to neutral. It is particularly suitable for broiling on pizzas or pastas, but when uncooked it is often used in salads or hors d'oeuvres. Tomatoes and mozzarella form a perfect duet. Mozzarella in brine, shrink-wrapped in foil, can be found in most grocery stores.

MASCARPONE: this soft, full-fat cream cheese is especially good in desserts and piquant sauces, though pasta dishes are also frequently improved with it. This cream cheese has a pleasant, mild, and sweet flavor, and gives off a wonderful odor of fresh cream. It comes from Lombardy and has a fat content of 60 percent dry weight.

You will find *mascarpone* in the iceboxes of larger supermarkets. It should always be refrigerated: after opening, reseal carefully, and replace immediately. Use quickly.

RICOTTA: This cream cheese, made from whey, is similar to low-fat farmer's cheese and is used in a similar way. It is produced throughout the whole of Italy, wherever cheese is made. *Ricotta* can be made from the whey of cow's milk, but also from goat's or ewe's milk. The name *ricotta* means "cooked again," and refers to the way it is produced. The cheese has a milky flavor that goes from mild and sour to a more subtle tartness. Its fat content is 20 percent dry weight. *Ricotta* can be used in many different ways: as a sandwich topping with sweet or piquant fillings (such as jam or herbs); together with *ruccola* in antipasti; and often as a filling for *cannelloni* or for sweet tarts and pastries.

Blue veined cheese

- GORGONZOLA: this world-famous, blue cream cheese is made from cow's milk and has a fat content of 48 percent dry weight. When young, it is called *dolce*. It then tastes spicy and piquant, but also has a discreet, sweet edge to it. It loses this as it ripens. The cheese then becomes stronger in flavor and has a hint of tartness. *Gorgonzola*, which originated in the eponymous Lombardy village north of Milan, was already being made a thousand years ago. These days, however, it tends to be produced in Lombardy and Piedmont. It is served as a table cheese and used to liven up sauces.

Homemade pasta

PASTA FROM YOUR OWN KITCHEN

For celebrity chefs and connoisseurs it is obvious: you make your own pasta. But even if this sounds as if it needs a lot of skill, producing your own pasta requires neither great culinary ingenuity nor any special ingredients.

The basic dough for pasta consists of flour, eggs, salt, and olive oil—all of which can be found in most kitchens anyway. The only other things you need to make your own pasta are time and labor, as preparing the pasta and then creating the shapes you desire cannot be rushed.

You can decide to go about the task in various ways. The easiest way is to make the pasta with a purpose-built machine. Preparing the basic pasta dough is not too difficult, though making perfect pasta shapes, creating for instance ringed pasta or well-proportioned ravioli, is of course a skill that develops with experience. The level of difficulty also increases somewhat if you want to dye the pasta. Still, it is always worth bearing in mind that master cooks are not made in heaven and that your results will continue to improve over time.

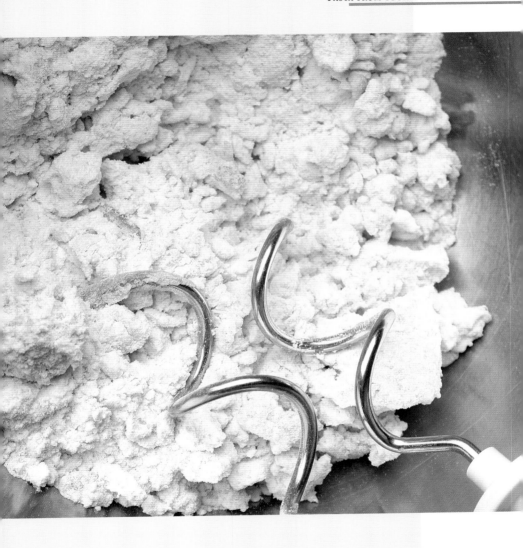

Kitchen Equipment

A QUICK START WITH STANDARD UTENSILS

For homemade pasta, you do not really require any special utensils. You will probably find all you need within your standard household equipment: scales, a blender or a hand mixer, knives, a rolling pin, and a pastry cutter.

If, however, you enjoy cooking pasta and do so frequently, you will find a whole range of special utensils commercially available—pasta machines first and foremost.

These kitchen aids are not all that expensive and enable you to roll the dough out flat on one side and then cut it into ribbon pasta on the other. With different settings or arrangements of the rollers, you can then create whatever shape of pasta you want, whether thin or broad.

For hand shaping, various small dough rollers are commercially available. The edges they create depend on the shape of the wheel: there are, for instance, rollers that produce a jagged edge.

For all who enjoy making their own pasta cases, special dough molds make things considerably easier. In these hinged molds, you first place the dough, then add a little filling and press the mold shut. This way you can get perfect ravioli, tortellini, or filled dumplings.

These molds are generally sold in sets that enable you to produce various different pasta cases—for instance, semicircular, rectangular, or even heart-shaped ones. Some of these sets can be surprisingly cheap.

Pasta Fatta in Casa

- INGREDIENTS (serves 6): 4 cups (500 g) flour, 1 tsp (5 g) salt, 5 eggs, 1 tbsp (15 ml) olive oil.

- 1. MIX THE FLOUR AND SALT. First sieve the flour onto a smooth work surface. Mix in the salt and make a hollow in the middle.

- 2. ADD THE EGGS AND OIL. Crack each egg individually and allow it to trickle into the hollow. Then slowly add a little oil. Gently stir the eggs and oil in the hollow with a fork.

3. MIX. Next, carefully blend all the ingredients, working from the outside in, until the eggs are thoroughly combined with the flour.

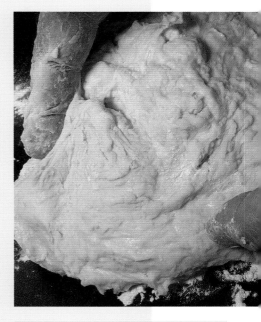

4. KNEAD. Now vigorously knead the dough until it is smooth and glossy. In order for the gluten in the flour to become active, you must knead the dough for at least five minutes. The dough must not be to sticky, nor too dry. For successful pasta, getting the right consistency of dough is crucial.

If the dough is too moist, it will not allow itself to be worked properly. To achieve the right consistency, you should if necessary knead in a little more flour. If the dough is too dry, add lukewarm water.

The kneading process is of the utmost importance, in order to produce an elastic dough that can be easily shaped. It is a good idea to test it after five or ten minutes: prod it with your finger and, if the dough springs back to its original shape, it has been sufficiently kneaded.

UTENSILS AND BOWLS FOR ALLOWING THE DOUGH TO REST

Kneading on a kitchen work surface is the classic way of producing pasta dough. Of course, you can always make your work easier by using a hand mixer and bowl. Put the ingredients into a bowl and knead the dough thoroughly with a dough hook.

5. LEAVE TO REST. Now the dough needs to rest for a good fifteen minutes. The best thing is to place it in paper towels that have been lightly dusted with flour. If you were to try and roll it out straightaway, it would still be too elastic. As it rests, the pasta dough becomes slightly dryer and softer. After allowing it to rest, give the dough another vigorous kneading.

Rolling out the pasta

Now the dough is ready to be turned into pasta. There are two basic methods. The simplest is to roll it out with a rolling pin and then shape the pasta with a pasta roller. This is suitable for broad-shaped pasta or when you want to work the dough to make ravioli or other pasta cases. The other alternative is to use a pasta machine.

In either case, first divide the dough into at least four smaller pieces and slap them down onto the worktop: the back of your hand should be held out broad and flat. The reason is that smaller pieces of dough are easier to roll.

1. ROLL THE DOUGH WITH THE ROLLING PIN. Working the dough with a rolling pin does take a little more time than processing it with a pasta machine, but it has the advantage of being easy to do.

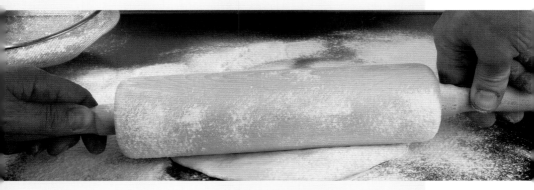

Squash one of the pieces of dough flat with your hand, and place it on a smooth work surface that has been coated with a thin layer of flour. With a rolling pin, roll the dough out thinly, working from center to edge. Take care not to roll beyond the edge of the dough, since it will then become too thin and you will not be able to work it easily. Scatter flour as necessary on the work surface and rolling pin, to prevent sticking. Then roll out the other dough pieces in the same way.

2. ROLLING DOUGH WITH A PASTA MACHINE. With any standard machine, it is possible to roll the dough out to whatever thickness you require, as the machine has two rollers opposite each other, the distance between which can be altered. For this purpose there is a small wheel at the side that you can adjust to various levels. To begin with, set the rollers as wide apart from one another as possible and then sprinkle them with a coating of flour. Then put each portion of dough twice through the machine.

When the dough has been squeezed through, pick it up in your hand and lay it flat on a wooden board dusted with flour. After it has been through the machine once, it should be soft and look silky. If the dough is too sticky, sprinkle it with a little flour.

STORING DOUGH PROPERLY

If the dough is not to be worked straightaway, or if you have to break for any reason, wrap the dough in a clean, dry dishtowel. Cover this dry towel with a second, moistened one. This will prevent the dough from drying out and disintegrating too quickly. If you need to interrupt your work for a longer period, it is a good idea to chill the dough. In this case, it must be brought back to room temperature before work is resumed on it.

Now adjust the settings on the machine so that the distance between the rollers is decreased by one notch. The dough goes through the rollers again and gets longer and thinner. Repeat the process until you reach the last-but-one setting on the pasta machine. By this stage, the dough will have the correct thickness for most purposes. For wafer-thin pasta, put the dough through one last time on the narrowest setting of the machine.

CUTTING THE PASTA INTO SHAPES

Now you can cut the pasta dough into the desired shapes.
Here, too, there are two possibilities. You can either use
a pasta cutter or knife, or make the pasta shapes with a pasta
machine. The latter, however, is relevant only if you are producing ribbon pasta.

- RIBBON PASTA. The rolled-out dough is cut up into
  rectangular pieces with a big knife. The length of the
  oblong thus determines the length of the pasta strips. If
  working with a pasta machine, the breadth of the dough
  should be measured to correspond to the breadth of
  the machine's rollers.

If working manually, use the pasta cutter to cut strips of dough that are, as far as possible, of equal breadth. Depending on the kind of cutter used, you can get different shaped edges—e.g., jagged.

If using a pasta machine, you can choose between different settings that will produce different breadths and shapes of pasta. In this way you can create any size and shape from thin spaghetti to broad ribbon pasta. After cutting, you can either continue to work the pasta or leave it to dry. Fresh pasta needs to be left to dry for a while (but no longer than 30 minutes) before being boiled.

The best way to dry ribbon pasta is on a wooden rod: the pasta is draped over it and hangs freely to dry. When completely dry, the pasta can be stored in an airtight container.

■ CANNELLONI AND LASAGNA. To cut out the somewhat bigger pasta shapes needed for lasagna or cannelloni, you can either use a sharp knife with a straight edge or a serrated pasta cutter. Cut the shapes to the length of lasagna that is going to be used, or into roughly 4 x 5 in (10 x 12 cm) pieces. These can be used both for lasagna and cannelloni.

SHORT COOKING TIME

Take care when cooking: homemade pasta is ready in about 3 minutes! The best thing is not to take your eyes off the pasta while it is on the burner. It is also a good idea to try it after a minute or two.

Before you can continue to work on the cut pasta, it must of course be dried. It is best to lay it out for several hours on a flat, level surface or gridiron.

■ FARFALLE. You can make this world-famous, butterfly-shaped pasta by cutting the rolled-out dough into squares of approximately 1 in (3 cm), using a serrated pasta cutter. Then pinch the center of each square into the shape of a bow tie.

IMAGINATIVE SHAPES FOR SPECIAL OCCASIONS

When shaping the pasta, you can also give free rein to your imagination. For instance, for a child's birthday you can create fairytale figures or imitate the shapes of toys. Pasta like this is particularly effective when dyed in pretty colors.

Dyeing pasta

DYEING AND FLAVORING PASTA

Dyed and flavored pasta can add variety to pasta cookery. As well as giving the most varied shapes and sizes to fresh pasta, there are also many ways in which you can spice them up to suit different tastes, or dye them different colors. In the end, there are no limits to the imagination.

SIMPLE WORK

Spicing or dyeing pasta does not require much ingenuity. You just need a little puréed beetroot, a pinch of saffron, or chopped spinach stirred into the pasta dough—and you will soon have the finest colored pasta. It is just as quick and easy to flavor the pasta—for example, with mushrooms or lemon.

To dye the pasta, first cook, then finely chop or purée, the required ingredients. These can then be added to the basic dough mix. Some should be mixed with the eggs in a bowl, but others can be blended into the dough later, when it is almost fully kneaded.

It is important to use the right amounts. Take special care when adding flavoring: you can have too much of a good thing, and end up spoiling the taste.

Whole-wheat pasta

Even the Italians are familiar with whole-wheat pasta, which they call *pasta integrale*. Whole-wheat pasta is mostly made from the flour or semolina of full, germinable corn, with or without eggs. But it can also be made from the flour of spelt, millet, buckwheat, amaranth, and rice.

So as to prevent the pasta from becoming too firm and heavy, some bran is generally sieved off after grinding—so much that out of 1 lb (400g) finely ground wheat, some 12 oz (300 g) flour is left. The bran is then used for baking bread. Of course, whole-wheat pasta in all its variety is in no way inferior to lighter sorts of pasta, but it is less often dyed. Since whole-wheat pasta breaks easily, however, it is most suitable for broad ribbon shapes or ravioli. Traditional recipes exist not only for whole-wheat pasta, but also for sauces that go especially well with it. Thanks to its strong, individual taste and porous surface, whole-wheat pasta is best suited to heavy, rich sauces.

Colored and flavored pasta

■ YELLOW PASTA. Grind one sachet (1 g) of saffron strands with a mortar and pestle and add to the flour with the eggs.

■ ORANGE PASTA. Use 3 tbsp (60 g) tomato paste plus 3 eggs and one yolk.

- RED PASTA. Use 1 small, cooked, and puréed beetroot plus 2 eggs and one yolk.

- GREEN PASTA. Use 10 oz (250 g) of blanched, well-squeezed, chopped spinach plus 2 eggs and 2 yolks.

- BOLETUS PASTA. Soak 2 tbsp (30 g) dried boletus mushrooms for 30 minutes in 4 tbsp (60 ml) freshly boiled water. Finely chop and add to the flour with the eggs.

- LEMON PASTA. Add 3 tbsp (45 g) of freshly grated lemon, orange, or sweet lime rind (unwaxed) to the pasta dough.

PASTA INTEGRALE (WHOLE-WHEAT PASTA WITHOUT EGGS)

INGREDIENTS (serves 4): 1¼ cups (250 g) whole-wheat flour; ½ tsp (2 g) sea salt; 2 tbsp (30 ml) olive oil; ½ cup (125 ml) lukewarm water.
Preparation time: about 1 hour.

Knead all the ingredients into a firm, smooth dough. Add the water very slowly, until the dough reaches the desired consistency. Then wrap the dough in flour-dusted paper towels and leave to rest for 10 minutes. Knead the dough thoroughly again and, if necessary, add a little water. Set aside for another 10 minutes. Now roll the dough out thinly on a flour-covered wooden board so that you can cut it into broad strips of ribbon pasta. Let the pasta dry for a while and then boil for about 5 minutes in plenty of salted water. The pasta is ready when it floats to the surface.

Filled pasta

PASTA TO SUIT YOUR OWN TASTE

Whether you want to make ravioli, tortellini with a spinach and ricotta filling, or cannelloni to your own recipe, making your own pasta cases and then filling them with whatever delicious ingredients you choose is by no means difficult.

The basic steps are always the same. First prepare your dough. While it is resting, get the filling ready—e.g., cook the ragú bolognese. The third step is to cut the pasta dough to size and stuff it with the prepared filling. Then fold up the pasta cases, seal the edges by moistening with water and pressing together with your fingers or a fork, and boil in salted water. You need to keep an eye on the pasta cases and ensure you boil them for the optimum time. The thickness of the dough is a decisive factor here.

SHAPING PASTA CASES

When producing your own pasta shapes, you have two alternatives: you can either prepare them entirely by hand or use special dough molds (see also p. 161). Both have their pros and cons. Handmade pasta cases, especially on their first boiling, look very "home-made" since you rarely get the edges exactly right. Of course, this has its own charm, since everyone can clearly see that what is being served has been freshly made by hand.

Even without much practice, you can achieve perfectly good results using molds. It is a quick and easy process. Once you have rolled out the pasta dough, cut it into shapes of the desired size. When working with molds, adjust the size of the pasta shapes accordingly—any superfluous material can be trimmed off once the mold is folded shut, then kneaded again and re-used.

For handmade tortellini, cut out circles about 2 in (5 cm) in diameter. Then add the filling to one half of the circle, and lightly brush the edge of the other half with water. Fold the moist edge onto the dry edge and press tightly together to make a crescent shape. Work this crescent into a circle and, where the pointed ends meet, moisten with a little water and press tight.

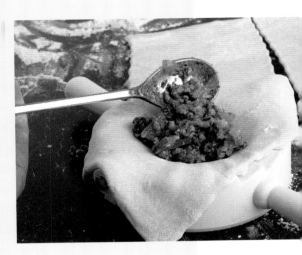

For ravioli, roll out two pieces of pasta dough into equal-sized rectangles. Place the filling on one piece of dough using a teaspoon, at intervals of about 1½ in (4cm). Brush the intervening spaces with a little water, then put the other layer of dough on top. Press together the areas of dough between the fillings and cut into squares. Then press together the edges of each square with a fork.

Gnocchi

A POTATO SPECIALTY

Gnocchi should not really enter the picture here, since they are a rather particular Italian pasta specialty. Unlike pasta they are not usually produced from flour or semolina, but from potatoes or choux pastry.

Throughout the region of the Alps, but especially in Piedmont, these curiously shaped little dumplings are very popular, being made exclusively out of mealy potatoes, flour, and salt. In the north, gnocchi are served with herbs, butter, and cheese; in Liguria, of course, with pesto; and, in the south, with tomato sauce.

In Verona, there is even a festival in honor of gnocchi, held on the last Friday of carnival; it is called *bacanal del gnoco* and involves a procession in historical

costume, leading the *papa del gnoco* to the cathedral. To round off the proceedings, plates full of gnocchi with a piquant sauce are served. Gnocchi go well with every sort of sugo and pesto, as well as tomato sauce, the juices from roast meat, grated hard cheese, or herbs sautéed in the finest olive oil. One real delicacy that should not be forgotten is gnocchi with white truffles, as served in Piedmont. In a well-stocked supermarket or Italian delicatessen you can purchase ready-made gnocchi, but you can easily make them yourself, too. It is not much more difficult than producing standard pasta dough out of flour and eggs in your own kitchen.

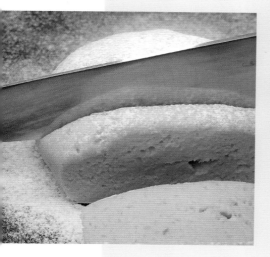

Gnocchi di patate alla piemontese

- INGREDIENTS (serves 6): for the dough: 2½ lb (1 kg) mealy potatoes; 2 cups (250g) flour; 1 tsp (5 g) salt. In addition: ½ bunch marjoram; 7 tbsp (100 g) butter; freshly grated parmesan. Preparation time: 1 hour 15 minutes.

- 1. BOIL THE POTATOES. Wash the potatoes and boil them in their skins for about 30 minutes, until soft. Peel.

- 2. RICE THE POTATOES. Press the still hot potatoes through a coarse sieve or potato ricer onto a lightly flour-coated worktop. Leave to cool for a while.

Types of potato

For successful gnocchi, the most important factor is the type of potato you use! Most suitable are the mealy varieties, as the dough must bind well.

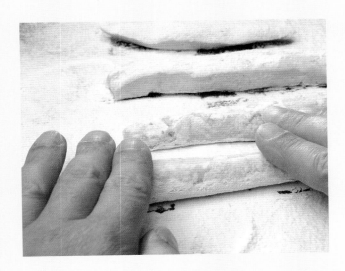

■ 3. KNEAD THE DOUGH. Now gradually mix the potatoes with the flour and salt and knead thoroughly until you get a smooth, homogenous dough. (It should not stick to your fingers.) Then shape the dough into a flattened hemisphere.

■ 4. CUT THE DOUGH. Cut the dough into approx ½ in wide (1 cm) slices, then into strips of ½ in (1 cm).

■ 5. ROLL THE DOUGH. Work the squares into little rolls on a flour-coated work surface.

■ 6. SHAPE THE GNOCCHI. Now the gnocchi can be shaped. You can do this in one of two ways: 1) cut the rolls into pieces 1–1½ in (2–3 cm) long and use the prongs of a fork to press them into shape; or 2) shape the dough in your hand with a little spoon. This requires a modicum of skill. Lay the prepared

gnocchi next to one another on flour-coated paper towels and set aside for about 15 minutes.

7. BOIL THE GNOCCHI. Meanwhile, bring 8 cups (2 liters) salted water to the boil in a big saucepan. Gradually pour the gnocchi into the water and cook over low heat for about 4 minutes. Stir carefully from time to time to prevent the gnocchi from sticking to each other. As soon as the little dumplings rise to the surface, remove them with a slotted spoon, and drain well.

8. SERVE. Sauté the herbs lightly in hot butter and pour over the gnocchi with plenty of grated parmesan.

SHORT COOKING TIME

Take care when cooking: homemade pasta is ready in about 3 minutes!

The great classics

THE GREAT CLASSICS

Despite the great variety of shapes and sizes, pasta is not all that is needed to create pasta cuisine. It becomes a real delicacy only when accompanied by a suitable sauce.

Pasta gained its worldwide popularity through a small number of different sauces—*bolognese*, *arrabiata*, *carbonara*, and *pesto* first and foremost. These great Italian classics have become well established and loved throughout the world.

SALSA AND SUGO

There are many basic types of Italian pasta sauce. For the meatless varieties, there are two approaches. First, there is salsa, which simply means "sauce;" and second, there is sugo, meaning "juice." The list of ingredients for salsa and sugo is endless. Many of them include tomatoes and vegetables such as olives, eggplants, zucchini, spinach, and even beans. So Italians use practically every type of vegetable for their sauces. A salsa can consist of one single kind of vegetable, or of several. The sauces are often given extra flavor by the addition of herbs and spices. Many are based on nuts, different types of cheese, or even lemons. But all sauces contain the finest cold-pressed olive oil or butter, and many of them also have cream.

Many variants

Just as there is no one single "pasta," there is no one single "sauce." Salsa and sugo, of course, vary from region to region, and from family to family.

The subtle differences between them arise, not just through the different preparation methods or quantities used, but also through the different ingredients. Even in the case of the great classics such as *ragout bolognese* and *pasta carbonara*, there is a great range of variants, all with very different tastes.

In Italy, indeed, there is a proverbial saying referring to this phenomenon, comparing a moody and capricious individual to a sauce: *cambia sempre come la salsa*—i.e., "he changes like the sauce."

Al aglio, olio e burro

Al aglio, olio e burro

10 min.

The authentic taste

The flavor of the pasta itself is, of course, best brought out when not drowned by a sauce. True, no pasta can do without additional ingredients (especially fats) to enliven its taste. So it should never be served completely on its own, but at its simplest either with olive oil (*olio*) or butter (*burro*). And do not forget the freshly grated hard cheese—parmesan is best. In Italy, the authentic taste of pasta is most commonly enjoyed with the addition of a little garlic and peperoncino too.

Aglio, olio e peperoncino

▬ INGREDIENTS (serves 4): 3 cloves garlic; ½ bunch flat-leaf parsley; 4 tbsp (60 ml) olive oil; 1 dried peperoncino; salt; freshly ground white pepper; freshly grated parmesan; 1½ lb (500 g) spaghetti.

▬ 1. COOK. Cook the spaghetti *al dente* in a big saucepan in bubbling salted water.

▬ 2. CHOP. Meanwhile, peel and halve the garlic cloves and finely chop the parsley.

3. SWEAT. Heat the oil in a large skillet and sweat the garlic and peperoncino over low heat. Remove the garlic and peperoncino from the pan and sprinkle the parsley into the oil.

4. MIX. Drain the spaghetti, mix well with the sautéed parsley, and season to taste with salt and pepper.

5. SERVE. Divide the pasta onto pre-heated plates, garnish with garlic and peperoncino, and serve. Sprinkle with freshly grated parmesan to taste.

VARIANTS

As far as being too spicy, this dish is pretty safe. If you prefer it with a bit of zing, just add more peperoncini.

Pesto

BASIL PESTO

One of the best-known accompaniments to pasta, and one of the best loved, is pesto—and it is quick and easy to prepare. The name "pesto" comes from *pestare*, meaning "to crush (as with a pestle)" or "to grind," alluding to the traditional way of preparing pesto, in which the ingredients (pine nuts, pecorino, parmesan, olive oil, garlic, and any quantity of basil) are crushed in a mortar.

These days, of course, a hand or electric blender can make the work much less onerous. With these, you can prepare *pesto* yourself in minutes.

Pesto is less a sauce in the usual sense—it is rather a spicy paste. Furthermore, it is always used cold and can sometimes be so dense that you need to stir a few spoonfuls of cooking water from the

pasta into it so as to produce the right consistency
for a sauce.

The original recipe
comes from Genoa, a fact
reflected in its traditional
designation *pasta alla genovese*. Even today, the
vast majority of Genoans
grow their own basil for
sauces.

READY-MADE PESTO FROM THE SUPERMARKET

Ready-made pesto, produced by various different manufacturers,
can be purchased from well-stocked supermarkets and specialty
shops. Their quality is of course quite variable.

Pesto alla genovese

Pesto is now enjoyed throughout Italy. This traditional pasta sauce from Liguria is also often used to spice up minestrone and other tasty soups.

- INGREDIENTS (serves 4): 4 big bunches basil; 3 cloves garlic; 4 oz (100 g) pine nuts; 2 oz (50 g) freshly grated parmesan or pecorino; 7 tbsp (100 ml) olive oil; salt.

- 1. WASH AND CHOP. First wash the basil and shake it dry. Peel the garlic and finely chop.

- 2. GRIND. Now put the basil, together with the chopped garlic and pine nuts, into a mortar and grind with a pestle. The order in which you add the ingredients is of no importance. To save time and effort, you can also use a blender to grind the ingredients. This is particularly easy to do when you have a so-called "universal blender" and a suitable fitting (see photos).

- 3. ADD CHEESE, OIL, AND SALT. When the ingredients have been sufficiently ground, first add the cheese and then, gradually, the oil. The pesto should eventually take on a slightly viscous consistency. The quantity of oil added is of decisive importance, so it is best not to add it all in one go, but spoon it in gradually, keeping a close eye on how the consistency is developing. Finally, add salt to taste.

STORING PESTO

Pesto can easily be made in great quantities and then stored in the refrigerator for several days. The most suitable is a jam jar that can be tightly sealed. To prevent the pesto from drying out, drizzle it with oil once it has been put in the jar.

Pesto

15 min.

Salsa di pomodori

TOMATO SAUCE

The pasta cuisine of Italy is unthinkable without freshly cooked tomato sauce—it is almost always needed. So most households keep the necessary ingredients on hand.

Salsa di pomodori is not used just in pasta dishes. It is also needed, for example, when preparing pizza, various different meat dishes, and fish stews. The absolute sine qua non here are tasty tomatoes that have ripened on the vine. Only they have the right note of fruity sweetness. Elongated plum tomatoes are the most suitable. In late summer, most Italian households stock up on the basic ingredients for making tomato sauce at home. Whole families even get together to cook pounds of tomatoes to a purée, called *passato*.

Outside the summer months, it is a good idea to use *pelati*—Italian canned tomatoes. The best come from the regions of Naples or Parma. Of course, it is also possible to use other canned tomatoes.

Salsa di pomodori

30 min.

INGREDIENTS (serves 4–6): 2½ lb (1 kg) ripe tomatoes; 1 carrot; 1 stick celery; 2 cloves garlic; 2 tbsp (30 ml) olive oil; 1 sprig fresh rosemary; 1 bunch basil; 1 pinch sugar; salt; freshly ground pepper.

1. SKIN AND CHOP. First, skin the tomatoes. To do this, make a cross-shaped cut into the skin, then blanch in boiling water. Plunge the tomatoes into cold water and remove the skin with a knife (see also p. 111). It is also possible to use canned, skinned tomatoes. Coarsely chop the tomatoes. Finely chop the carrot, celery, and garlic.

2. SAUTÉ LIGHTLY AND COOK. Sauté the vegetables in the heated oil. They should take on just a hint of color and not be allowed to brown too much. Add the tomatoes and spices. Cook over medium heat for about 30 minutes. The sauce should eventually have the consistency of mush and be quite viscous.

3. PURÉE. Press the sauce through a sieve, or purée it in a blender, and mix in the chopped basil.

Salsa di besciamella

BÉCHAMEL SAUCE

Béchamel sauce is the classic sauce for a variety of broiled pasta dishes. The basic preparation is similar to that of a roux or light sauce.

■ INGREDIENTS (serves 4–6): 4 tbsp. (60 g) butter; ¼ cup (60 g) flour; 1 cup (250 ml) milk; salt; freshly ground pepper; grated nutmeg.

■ 1. MELT THE BUTTER. First melt the butter in a saucepan over medium heat until it starts to foam. Do not allow it to brown.

■ 2. SWEAT THE FLOUR. Now add the flour and lightly sauté until it turns golden yellow. This is best done with a whisk.

■ 3. ADD MILK. Now slowly add the milk, stirring constantly. Make sure no little lumps form. The best way to prevent this is simply to keep stirring.

4. SIMMER. Now let the sauce simmer over low heat for at least 10 minutes, until it thickens and no longer tastes mealy.

5. FLAVOR. When the *salsa besciamella* is ready, add salt, pepper, and a generous pinch of nutmeg to taste.

Salsa di besciamella

 20 min.

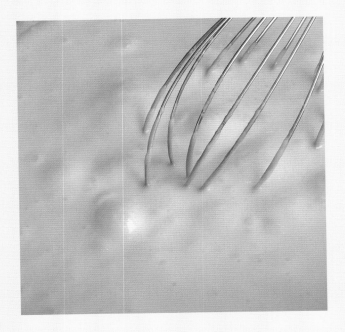

Ragù bolognese

MEAT SAUCE

Spaghetti bolognese—this must be the best-known pasta dish in the whole world. Of course, the basic sauce can be served, not just with spaghetti, but also for instance with tagliatelle or macaroni, or even worked into lasagna (see p. 218).

Given the great popularity of this sauce even outside Italy, it is no wonder that it comes in many different forms. The basic recipe originated in Bologna, as its name indicates. Here, the sauce is cooked with a mixture of chicken liver and ground meat. But *pasta bolognese* can of course also be cooked without liver and made, for example, with ground beef. Other cooks leave out the celery and thicken the sauce with cream.

When all is said and done, the main rule with this dish is: prepare it whichever way you prefer! Or rather: if it tastes good, that is the right way to cook it!

▬ INGREDIENTS (serves 4–6): 1 onion; 1 carrot; 1 stick celery; 2 oz (50 g) pancetta (or, if preferred, streaky bacon); 2 tbsp (30 ml) olive oil; 1 lb (400 g) mixed ground meat (beef/pork); ½ cup (125 ml) dry white wine; ½ cup (125 ml) meat stock; 1½ lb (500 g) skinned tomatoes; salt; freshly ground pepper.

▬ 1. CHOP. First peel the onion, carrot, and celery, then wash and dice. Cut the pancetta into small cubes.

▬ 2. SAUTÉ LIGHTLY. Now sauté the vegetables lightly in the heated oil. Add the pancetta and fry until glazed.

▬ 3. FRY. Add the ground meat. Stirring and turning constantly, fry until it disintegrates into little pieces.

4. SEASON AND ALLOW TO SIMMER. Add the wine, stock, and tomatoes, season to taste, cover, and allow to simmer for about 30 minutes.

FRESH HERBS

The savor of a ragú bolognese can be enhanced by fresh herbs, for example a sprig of rosemary, added to the mixture as it simmers.

Ragù bolognese

 45 min.

Alfredo

Alfredo

15 min.

CREAM SAUCE

Rich—and at first glance not typically Italian—this simple cream sauce is a nice and rather different alternative to the well-known salsas and sugi. So salsa di alfredo enjoys great popularity throughout Italy and, in different guises, is often used as the basis for vegetable sauces: e.g., with mushrooms. One of its great advantages is that it is very quick and easy to prepare—the sauce is ready to be served straightaway with pasta.

■ INGREDIENTS (serves 4–6): scant stick (100 g) butter; 6 oz (150 g) freshly grated parmesan; 1½ cups (350 ml) light cream; 1 bunch flat-leaf parsley; salt; freshly ground pepper; 1½ lb (500 g) pasta; fresh thyme to garnish.

■ 1. COOK THE PASTA. Cook the pasta *al dente* in a big saucepan of bubbling, salted water.

■ 2. THICKEN THE SAUCE. At the same time, melt the butter in a skillet and add the parmesan and cream, stirring constantly over low heat. Allow the sauce to thicken slightly.

3. SEASON. Now add the parsley, season the sauce with salt and pepper to taste, and stir well.

4. MIX. Drain the pasta and keep it warm in a saucepan. Add the sauce and mix together well.

IMPROVE ITS APPEARANCE

Salsa di alfredo is light and relatively colorless. When you want to create a feast for the eyes too, it is a good idea to use colored pasta to brighten up the meal a little. Red pasta works well. Fresh herbs such as thyme, rosemary, or basil are very suitable for the garnish.

Napolitana

TOMATO AND CELERY SAUCE

The basic recipe for this sauce comes from Naples, where it is enjoyed not only on pasta, but also, for instance, on a freshly baked pizza.

- INGREDIENTS (serves 4–6): 2 tbsp (30 ml) olive oil; 1 onion; 1 carrot; 1 stick celery; 1½ lb (500 g) tomatoes; 1 bunch flat-leaf parsley; 2 tbsp (30 g) sugar; ½ cup (120 ml) water; salt; freshly ground black pepper; 1½ lb (500 g) pasta; fresh herbs to garnish.

- 1. CHOP. Cut the tomatoes, vegetables, and parsley into pieces and chop finely.

- 2. SAUTÉ. Heat the oil in a pan and lightly sauté the onion, carrot, and celery over low heat for about 10 minutes until soft. Stir frequently.

- 3. SIMMER. Add the tomatoes, parsley, sugar, and water and bring to a boil. Lower the temperature and cover. Allow to simmer for about 45 minutes.

KEEPING SAUCE IN RESERVE:

If you cook it for longer, you will get a more concentrated sauce that is easy to freeze. So it is well worth cooking this sauce in large quantities. After thawing, you simply pour stock over the sauce, or thin it with water.

Napolitana

1,5 uur

- 4. COOK THE PASTA. In good time, before the sauce has finished cooking, cook the pasta *al dente* in a big saucepan full of bubbling, salted water.

- 5. TASTE AND SERVE. Season with salt and black pepper to taste. Drain the pasta and divide between pre-warmed plates. Add the sauce and garnish with fresh herbs as desired.

Carbonara

HAM AND CREAM SAUCE

This sauce is also one of the great classics of international cooking. It is particularly popular in Germany, for example, where it has long been a symbol of Italian cookery. As with most other widespread dishes, variants are frequently encountered. It is the use of ham that gives this sauce its distinctive taste. In Italy, the type generally used is *pancetta*, but *carbonara* can also be made from other types of cooked (and even uncooked) ham or bacon.

Carbonara

40 min.

- INGREDIENTS (serves 4–6): 8 oz (200 g) pancetta; 4 eggs; 2 oz (50 g) freshly grated parmesan; 1½ cups (400 ml) light cream; salt; freshly ground pepper; 1½ lb (500 g) pasta.

- 1. FRY. First cut the pancetta into small cubes. Then fry until crispy in a skillet, over medium heat, taking care that it does not burn. Drain on paper towels.

- 2. COOK THE PASTA. Cook the pasta *al dente* in a big saucepan of boiling, salted water.

3. PREPARE THE EGGS AND CREAM. Beat the cream, eggs, and parmesan thoroughly together in a bowl.

4. SIMMER. Pour the egg and cream mixture into a pan and cook until it has thickened. Then stir in the pancetta and season with black pepper to taste.

5. MIX WELL. Drain the pasta and keep it warm in the saucepan. Pour the sauce over the pasta and carefully stir together.

Putanesca

Putanesca

⏳ 40 min.

SAUCE WITH OLIVES AND ANCHOVIES.

Outside Italy, this sauce, with its distinctive taste of ripe olives and flavorsome anchovy fillets, is not as well known as bolognese or carbonara. In its motherland, however, putanesca is a classic and highly prized.

▬ INGREDIENTS (serves 4): 2 tbsp (30 ml) olive oil; 3 cloves garlic; 1 bunch flat-leaf parsley; 1 peperoncino; 1½ lb (500 g) fresh (or canned) tomatoes; 1 tbsp (15 g) capers; 3 anchovy fillets; 3½ tbsp (50 g) black pitted olives; freshly ground black pepper; freshly grated parmesan; 1½ lb (500 g) pasta.

▬ 1. CHOP. Squash the garlic cloves with a knife held slantwise. Finely chop the parsley and peperoncini. Blanch and skin the tomatoes (see p. 111), remove the core and seeds, and cut the flesh into small cubes. Cut the anchovy fillets into small pieces.

▬ 2. COOK THE PASTA. Cook the pasta *al dente* in a big saucepan of boiling, salted water.

3. SAUTÉ. Meanwhile, heat the oil in a saucepan. Lightly sauté the garlic, parsley, and peperoncini for about 1 minute, stirring constantly.

4. SEASON. Add the tomatoes and bring to the boil. Cover and simmer over low heat for about 5 minutes. Add the capers and olives and simmer for another 5 minutes.

5. TASTE. Add black pepper to taste.

6. SERVE. Pour out the pasta and drain. Divide among pre-warmed plates, pour the sauce over the pasta, and add the anchovies. Serve straightaway with grated parmesan.

Arrabiata

Arrabiata

40 min.

SAUCE WITH PEPERONCINI

Do you need to spice things up a bit? Then arrabiata is for you! The peperoncini give this sauce its distinctive taste, and the more chilies you add, the hotter the pasta dish will be.

- INGREDIENTS (serves 4): 4 oz (100 g) pancetta; 3 red peperoncini; 1 large onion; 1 clove garlic; 1½ lb (500 g) tomatoes; ½ cup (120 ml) water; 1 bunch flat-leaf parsley; salt; freshly ground pepper; freshly grated pecorino; 1½ lb (500 g) pasta.

- 1. CHOP. Finely chop the pancetta, peperoncini, onion, garlic, and parsley. Blanch and skin the tomatoes (see p. 111), then chop into small pieces.

- 2. SAUTÉ. Cook the pancetta in a skillet. Add the onion, garlic, and peperoncini and lightly sauté over medium heat until brown, stirring several times.

- 3. SIMMER. Add the tomatoes and water. Cover, and simmer over low heat until the sauce has reached a thick, creamy consistency.

4. COOK THE PASTA. Meanwhile, cook the pasta in a big saucepan full of boiling, salted water. Drain well, and keep warm in the pan.

5. SEASON AND SERVE. Stir the parsley into the sauce and season to taste. Pour the sauce over the pasta and mix carefully. Add freshly grated pecorino and serve.

PROTECTING THE HANDS

When chopping chilies, it is a good idea to wear rubber gloves, as they will protect your hands from any irritation. The peperoncini can otherwise "burn" sensitive skins.

Marinara

SEAFOOD SAUCE

In all places around the Mediterranean, seafood sauces naturally form part of a cook's repertoire. You will find no fishing village or coastal resort where marinara does not feature on the pasta menu.

What exactly comprises a classic *marinara*, however, is difficult to say. For centuries, Italian cooks have worked with whatever could be freshly fished—for example, octopus, squid, mussels, crabs, scampi, clams, and whiting. There are no "exact" recipes for a *marinara*. So from one region, village, or kitchen to another, quite different sauces are prepared, all with completely different tastes.

Which seafood you choose for your sauce is thus down to individual taste—or whatever is available on the fresh fish counter at the time. Tinned seafood can also be used, if preferred.

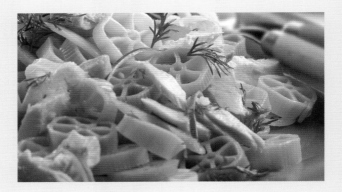

The recipe below comes from southern Italy and contains, not just seafood, but fish fillets too.

- INGREDIENTS (serves 4): 2 tbsp (30 ml) olive oil; 1 onion; 2 cloves garlic; ½ cup (120 ml) red wine; 2 tbsp (40 g) tomato paste; 1½ lb (500 g) tomatoes; 1 small bunch basil; 1 small bunch oregano; 12 mussels; 2 tbsp (30 g) butter; 5 oz (120 g) squid; 5 oz (120 g) filleted whiting or cod; 8 oz (200 g) shrimp (shelled); salt; freshly ground pepper; 1½ lb (500 g) pasta.

- 1. CHOP AND WASH. Wash the mussels and remove their beards. Finely chop the onion and herbs. Blanch and skin the tomatoes (see p. 111), remove the cores and seeds, and cut the flesh into small cubes. Cut the fish fillets into small pieces.

- 2. SAUTÉ. Heat the olive oil in a large saucepan, add the onion and garlic, and brown over low heat.

3. SIMMER. Pour in the wine with the tomatoes and tomato paste and simmer for about 10 minutes over medium heat, until the sauce has thickened slightly. Stir several times.

4. SEASON. Stir the herbs into the sauce and season to taste with salt and pepper. Keep warm.

5. COOK THE MUSSELS. Meanwhile, heat a sufficient quantity of water and boil the mussels for about 5 minutes, until they open. Take the mussels out, discard any that are still closed, and set the others aside. Add some of the cooking water from the mussels to the tomato sauce and bring to the desired consistency.

6. SAUTÉ THE FISH. Melt the butter in a skillet and sauté the squid, fish fillets, and shrimp in succession for 1 to 2 minutes, until soft. Add to the warm tomato sauce and stir.

7. COOK THE PASTA. While cooking the mussels, cook the pasta *al dente* in a big saucepan full of bubbling, salted water. Drain well.

8. MIX. Mix the sauce into the pasta, add the mussels, and serve.

Marinara

60 min.

Lasagne al forno

Of all the Italian dishes in which pasta is baked in the oven, lasagne al forno is one of the most famous. The filling of ragú bolognese and the layered construction of pasta make it popular with everybody, young and old.

The word *lasagne* designates the layered pasta and the way it is baked with béchamel sauce and cheese. Only when a *ragú bolognese* filling is used do we have a *lasagne al forno*.

MANY DIFFERENT VARIANTS

This is, of course, just one way of cooking with lasagna. There are many different fillings for the layers of pasta. Especially delicious are the vegetarian dishes—fillings of spinach or broccoli, mushrooms or bell pepper. In fact, you can bake any pre-cooked vegetable in this way. In addition, you can also use other types of meat (e.g., poultry). Fillings of fish or seafood are also possible.

■ INGREDIENTS (serves 4): 16 sheets lasagna; *ragú bolognese* (see p. 200); *salsa besciamella* (see p. 198); 6 oz (150 g) mozzarella; 4 oz (100 g) freshly grated parmesan; 1 tbsp (15 g) butter.

1. PREPARE THE SAUCE. For *lasagne al forno* you
need *ragú bolognese* for the filling and béchamel sauce for
baking. Both sauces should be cooked before the lasagna
is prepared.

2. CUT. Cut the mozzarella into small cubes.

3. PREPARE. Set out the lasagna sheets, cheese, and
both sauces. Oil a big, flameproof baking pan.

4. LAYER. Cover the base of the baking pan with
béchamel sauce and place a few lasagna sheets in it. Cover
with a little *ragú*, pour béchamel sauce on top, and cover
with more layers of pasta. Continue until all the ingredi-

Lasagne al forno

120 min.

ents have been used. The last layer should consist of béchamel sauce.

5. OVERLAY WITH CHEESE. Scatter the mozzarella over the sauce, sprinkle with parmesan, and dot with butter.

6. BAKE. Preheat the oven to 400 °F (200 °C). Bake the lasagna for about 40 minutes, until an attractive, golden-brown crust has formed.

Ready-made pasta layers

Even with lasagna, freshly prepared pasta tastes best. You can, however, also use the packaged sort. There are many different types: some still need to be pre-cooked, while others are ready for layering. Instant lasagna sheets need plenty of sauce, of course, since they absorb a great deal of liquid.

Regional specialties

Liguria

THE CUISINE OF RETURNING TRAVELERS

Cucina del ritorno ("the cuisine of returning travelers") is the nickname given to Ligurian cooking. It alludes to the yearnings felt by seafarers of earlier times for the smell of herbs and the greenery of the vegetable fields on the narrow, sun-ripened stretches of coastline in the northwest of Italy. The Ligurian coast is distinguished by fishing and the cultivation of olives, but most particularly by the intensive use of herbs for seasoning. There is no dish without herbs—for one famous example, you need only think of pesto.

Pesto tastes better in Liguria than anywhere else, as Ligurian basil is a small-leaved, especially flavorsome variety. Ligurians use *pesto* in three different ways: in vegetable-rich minestrone, as a seasoning that melts on hot ribbon pasta, and as a sauce for Genovese gnocchi.

Another particularity of the region is the highly aromatic Ligurian olive oil. It is one of the best of its kind in Italy. In countless small presses, the "liquid gold of Liguria" (as it is called) is produced in a highly elaborate procedure.

In other regards, the cooking of Liguria is distinguished by a subtle simplicity. Ordinary ingredients are usually prepared with love and labor, as in the case (for example) of the famous *ravioli alla genovese*. This has a long history behind it—the pasta cases, artfully filled, were already very popular in the Middle Ages.

RAVIOLI ALLA GENOVESE

■ INGREDIENTS (serves 6): for the pasta dough: 3½ cups (400 g) flour; 4 eggs; salt. For the filling: 6 oz (150 g) minced veal; 4 oz (100 g) sweetbreads; 4 oz (100 g) veal sausage meat; 1 small, stale loaf of bread; 8 oz (200 g) Swiss chard leaves; 5 oz (125 g) borage; 2 eggs; 3 tbsp (45 g) freshly grated parmesan; salt; freshly ground pepper. To serve: 5 tbsp (75 g) melted butter; plenty of fresh thyme; 5 tbsp (75 g) freshly grated parmesan.

■ 1. PREPARE THE DOUGH. See basic recipe on p. 162.

■ 2. PREPARE THE VEGETABLES. Wash the chard and borage leaves and remove their stems. Blanch in boiling, salted water for about 3 minutes. Rinse with cold water. Drain, press well, and finely chop. It is best to place the vegetables in a dish and set them aside.

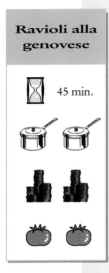

Ravioli alla genovese

45 min.

3. DICE THE SWEETBREADS. Blanch the sweetbreads in boiling water for 5 minutes, then plunge in cold water. Remove the skin and blood vessels, and chop into very small cubes. Add to the vegetables.

4. SOAK THE LOAF. Rub the crust off the loaf and soak the soft inside for about 10 minutes in lukewarm water. Squeeze out the excess water and break the bread in pieces with a fork.

5. MIX THE FILLING. Add the minced veal and sausage meat to the vegetables in the bowl. Stir in 2 eggs, the bread, and the parmesan, using a wooden spoon to mix them to a smooth, pliable consistency. Season with salt and pepper. The filling should be well bound, but moist. If it is too runny, add a few breadcrumbs and grated parmesan. If too dry, mix in an egg yolk.

6. CUT OUT THE RAVIOLI SHAPES AND FILL THEM. Now divide the ball of pasta dough into two halves and roll each half out thinly on a surface lightly sprinkled with flour. Use a dough cutter to cut into an even number of strips 2 in (5 cm) wide. Place a teaspoon of filling at 1½ in (3 cm) intervals on half of the strips. Then lay the remaining strips of dough over them; it is now just a matter of cutting out the ravioli. Do not forget to press the edges lightly together and close the cases by pushing down with a fork all the way round, so they will stay in one piece throughout cooking. Before cooking, the ravioli should be laid out on a flour-covered dishtowel and briefly dried.

7. COOK THE RAVIOLI. Place the ravioli in 12 cups (3 liters) bubbling, salted water and cook for about 3 minutes. The water does not need to be boiling—it is enough for the ravioli to rise to the surface and cook there.

8. SERVE. Finally, melt the butter and add the finely chopped thyme. Drain the ravioli thoroughly, drizzle the thyme butter over the ravioli, and serve with freshly grated parmesan.

Piedmont and Val d'Aosta

COOKING WITH THE FINEST INGREDIENTS

Piedmont has scenery straight out of a picture book: dominated by the Alps, but with rich, rolling hills of incredible beauty as well, all of them surrounded by vines. Added to this are all those picturesque localities with their medieval towns and castles.

Piedmont cuisine can only be described as highly refined. It is in the region around Alba that you will find the most expensive and elegant of mushrooms, namely truffles—particularly the white kind. The fruit from Piedmont is something special too—you need only think of Piedmont cherries.

But however aristocratic things may appear, it is not always like this in Piedmont. Apart from the truffles, which are indeed a rather exclusive item, northern Italian cookery was originally that of poor people. It was—and still is—closely linked with the earth and its fruits.

The rich and varied ingredients provided by Mother Nature are here turned into simple, but incredibly tasty, dishes thanks to the creativity of local cooks. Chief among them is the Piedmont national dish, *bagna cáuda*. This vegetable fondue, in which fresh vegetables are dipped in a hot sauce of anchovies, garlic, and oil, is still served today. It is always made, for example, when the grape harvest comes to an end and the families of grape pickers gather together to celebrate.

In other ways, meals in northern Italy generally tend to be hearty affairs. In many places you will find pasta variations with strong sauces, potato gnocchi, lima beans, salami, and wild boar. The more you move northward into the barren mountains of the Val d'Aosta, the cuisine becomes correspondingly less varied. But for just that same reason, it becomes hearty, filling, and rich in calories. Meals in the Val d'Aosta generally begin with bread soup and cheese, with smoked bacon, butter, and cream being used in great quantities. Then you get fine dishes of freshwater fish, as the glaciers

EXCHANGE AND BARTER

How is it that anchovies form part of *bagna cáuda*, the national dish of winegrowers in Piedmont? The answer is simple: from the earliest times there was a lively trade with peasants on the Ligurian coasts, who exchanged their anchovies for butter, cheese, and wheat.

of the huge peaks surrounding the Val d'Aosta (Mont Blanc, the Matterhorn, and Monte Rosa) can fill fishermen's nets from their abundant rivers.

FETTUCCINE WITH WHITE TRUFFLES

- INGEDIENTS (serves 4): for the sauce: 4 cups (500 ml) light cream; 2 red chillies; 1 tsp (5 ml) truffle oil; salt; freshly ground white pepper. In addition: 4 tbsp (60 g) white truffle shavings; 1 tbsp (15 g) chopped basil; freshly grated parmesan; 1½ lb (600 g) fettuccine.

- 1. CHOP. Cut up the chillies, remove the seeds and ribs, and slice into narrow strips.

- 2. COOK THE CREAM SAUCE. Reduce the cream to about half its volume in a saucepan. Turn down the heat and stir in the truffle oil and chillies. Season the cream sauce with salt and pepper.

- 3. COOK THE PASTA. Cook the fettuccine *al dente* in a big saucepan of bubbling, salted water and drain.

- 4. ADD THE TRUFFLES AND SERVE. Divide the pasta between pre-warmed plates and pour on the sauce. Then add the truffles in wafer-thin shavings. [N.B: immediately before you slice the truffles, rinse them in cold, running water and dry on paper towels. It is essential that the truffles do not absorb any of the water. Grimy recesses can be carefully cut away with a sharp pointed knife.] Sprinkle the dish with basil and parmesan, and serve immediately.

Fettuccine with white truffles

30 min

Lombardy

OPULENT SPECIALTIES

As in the whole of northern Italy, meals are rather opulent affairs: butter, cream, and gorgonzola are popular ingredients. Unlike in the rest of Italy, however, it was not pasta that played the main role here, but rice.

As far as cooks in Lombardy are concerned, you cannot do anything without butter and rice, which are central to most dishes. The first fields of rice were already being planted here in the 15th century. A distinction was drawn early on in the Po Valley between Japanese and Indian rice: it was the Japanese variety that was most probably responsible for the types of rice that are harvested these days—*baldo*, *arborio*, and *carnaroli*, for instance. Japanese rice suited the climate best and led to good harvests. The center of Lombardy cuisine is the vibrant metropolis of Milan, surrounded by the fertile Po plain in which pretty much everything will grow. Next to rice, it is Lombardy's second specialty, the blue-veined cream cheese gorgonzola, that is most prized here—it was discovered in the place of the same name. It also plays the main role in most of the region's pasta dishes—either as a central element in *sugo* or combined with other types of cheese. There are countless variants, one of them in combination with ham.

As a main course, there is one classic dish in particular that has become famous far and wide: *osso buco*, knuckle of veal with bone marrow stewed in a ragout. Beef is eaten just as much in Lombardy, too. Trout from Lake Como or Lake Maggiore appear only further down the menu.

The most famous dessert of Lombardy is *panettone*, a yeast cake with raisins and fruit that is mainly served at yuletide.

PASTA AL GORGONZOLA

Pasta al gorgonzola

30 min.

■ INGREDIENTS (serves 4); for the sauce: 8 oz (200 g) gorgonzola; 1 tbsp (15 ml) olive oil; 1 small onion; 1 clove garlic; 1½ cups (400 ml) light cream; a few leaves of sage; ground white pepper; 1½ lb (500 g) dyed pasta.

■ 1. CHOP. First remove the rind from the gorgonzola and cut the cheese into cubes. Finely chop the onion and garlic. Cut the sage leaves into strips.

■ 2. HEAT THE ONION AND THE GARLIC. Now heat the oil in a saucepan and sauté the chopped onion and garlic until they are glazed.

■ 3. COOK THE SAUCE. Add cream, sage, and gorgonzola and cook over low heat, stirring constantly, until the cheese has melted. Season with salt and pepper.

■ 4. COOK THE PASTA. Meanwhile, cook the pasta *al dente* in a big saucepan full of bubbling salted water.

■ 5. MIX AND SERVE. Drain the pasta, mix in the gorgonzola sauce, and serve immediately while still hot. Since the sauce already includes cheese, there is no need to serve parmesan as well.

South Tyrol and Trentino

As is the case with all border territories, the autonomous province of the South Tyrol is distinguished by a culture (and a culinary culture too) that represents a crossover from one country to another. In particular, dumplings, bacon, and thick noodles made of potato, flour, and egg all go to show that dishes from Austria have managed to cross the border into Italy. And vice versa, too: north of the Alps, cooks can take advantage of the extensive fruit cultivation in the climatically well-favored

region of the South Tyrol. Fruit, especially apples, is found here in abundance. At harvest time, whole families climb up trees on their rickety ladders. In spring, the hillsides gleam with the fragrant white and delicate pink of the blossoming trees. Even grapevines find the conditions here suit them.

But even though the spring in the South Tyrol and Trentino is very mild, winters are long and severe. So hearty, filling, and calorie-rich dishes are typical of the Alpine regions—bread, cheese, and cream are always included.

The slaughter of pigs in November and December enables the hill farmers to lay in a provision of dried meat for the winter. The air-dried ham made in this region is a particular specialty.

At lower altitudes, especially the Trentino, vegetables grow in great abundance. Vegetable markets in the towns and cities are a feast for the eyes. Thus there is a rich variety of vegetarian dishes. There are also a few culinary creations involving freshwater fish, such as trout and whitefish, from the clear mountain streams and many lakes—though these are not quite so dominant on menus.

SPINACH IN PASTA

■ INGREDIENTS (serves 4): for the dough: ½ cup (125 g) rye flour; 1 cup (125 g) wheat flour; 1 egg; salt; 1 tbsp (15 ml) olive oil. For the filling: 1 lb (400 g) fresh spinach; 4 tbsp (60 g) chopped parsley; 1 onion; ½ cup (120 g) butter; 1 tbsp (15 g) flour; ½ cup (125 ml) milk; 3½ tbsp (50 g) parmesan; salt; pepper; nutmeg.

Spinach in pasta

75 min.

1. MAKE THE DOUGH. Knead the flour, egg, salt, and oil into a dough, if necessary adding a little lukewarm water.

2. PREPARE THE SPINACH. Wash the spinach and cook in boiling, salted water. Rinse in cold water, drain, thoroughly squeeze out the excess water, and finely chop. Mix with the parsley.

3. MAKE THE FILLING. Chop the onion into small pieces and briefly brown in 4 tsp (20 g) butter. Coat with a little flour and add the milk. Stir well and reduce a little. Add the spinach and season to taste with salt, pepper, and nutmeg. Stir in 1 tbsp (15 g) parmesan and allow the filling to cool.

4. PREPARE THE DOUGH. Roll the dough out thinly and cut out round pieces 3–4 in (8–10 cm) using a round object—a wide, upended glass is ideal. Keep working the dough continuously, so that it does not dry out.

5. FILL THE CASES. Place the filling onto the dough pieces with a little spoon, fold them into crescent shapes, and seal the edges firmly.

6. COOK AND SERVE. Cook the spinach in pasta for 5 minutes in bubbling, salted water. Melt the remaining butter. Serve the pasta cases on plates or in a bowl, drizzle the melted butter over, and add a sprinkling of fresh parmesan.

Emilia-Romagna

THE LAND OF SPECIALTIES

The richest and most varied cuisine in the whole of Italy is definitely that of Emilia-Romagna. Most specialties that are famed and popular in other countries originate in this region.

These specialties include the fine, tangy *aceto balsamico* that matures for between 12 and 25 years in vats of varying size and wood types; Parma ham, prized throughout the world; *mortadella* and many other varieties of sausage; and (last but not least) the celebrated *parmigiano reggiano*, that hard cheese that is a must with almost every pasta dish.

Bologna is the capital city of this region: its nickname is *la grassa*, meaning "fat," "sumptuous," or "rich." From Bologna also comes *ragú bolognese*, one of the most famous, if not *the* most famous of all pasta sauces with meat. And the filled rings of pasta known as *tortellini* also play an

important role in Bologna: traditionally they are eaten as an appetizer to the Christmas meal, though nobody knows for sure whether they were actually invented here or not. In fact, Emilia-Romagna is home to a great variety of pasta dishes. It is, as it were, the motherland of homemade pasta—lasagna, tagliatelle, and so on. For people still make their own pasta, at least on a Sunday. Of course, the pasta here is mainly made from wheat flour and eggs, while in the south it is made almost exclusively from milled durum and water. Pasta fillings and sauces usually contain meat, especially ham, or parmesan, or ricotta. Everything is prepared with patience, taking plenty of time, and the cuisine is rich and substantial—hardly anyone can resist it.

PENNE AL PROSCIUTTO

- INGREDIENTS (serves 4–6): 6 oz (150 g) Parma ham; 3½ tbsp (50 g) freshly grated parmesan; 1 small onion; 3½ tbsp (50 g) melted butter; salt; freshly ground pepper; 1½ lb (500 g) penne.

- 1. COOK THE PASTA. Bring 12 cups (3 liters) salted water to a boil in a big saucepan and cook the pasta *al dente*.

- 2. CHOP THE HAM. Cut the ham into small cubes, separating the fat from the lean. Finely chop the onion.

- 3. SAUTÉ LIGHTLY. Heat the butter in a large pan, add the fat from the ham, and lightly brown. Then add the onion and sauté until glazed. Stir in the cubes of lean ham and continue to sauté, stirring constantly.

- 4. MIX. Drain the penne well and add to the pan. Mix together thoroughly and season with salt and pepper.

- 5. SERVE. Divide the pasta between warmed plates and sprinkle with freshly grated parmesan.

Penne al prosciutto

20 min.

OTHER TYPES OF HAM

If you cannot get hold of Parma ham, you can of course use other types, though the authentic taste of this dish will then be lost.

Veneto and Friuli

CUISINE OF INTERNATIONAL DISTINCTION

The cooking of the Veneto is considered to be refined, light, and easy to digest. It is distinguished, after all, by two geographical factors: the sea with its associated fishing activities on the one side and the plain of the Po with its numerous rice fields on the other.

As the leading trading center on the Mediterranean, Venice was naturally the first European city to come into contact with exotic spices and fruits from overseas—so these ingredients are naturally found in many of its recipes. The Veneto is divided into a mountainous region in the north, extending as far as the Austrian border, and a broad, flat plain in the south. It is considered to be among the most developed culinary regions of Italy. Its menus include many famous delicacies, such as Venetian guinea fowl, and the firm, red, and slightly bitter vegetable used in salads that is known as *radicchio di Treviso*.

One Venetian specialty is hearty spaghetti made from whole-wheat flour, called *bigoli*. This has always been served in the Veneto on fasting days such as Ash Wednesday or Good Friday. It traditionally comes with a sauce of anchovies, onions, and olive oil. These days, whole-wheat spaghetti is also enjoyed with braised quail or guinea fowl.

In Friuli, just to the east, you can already sense the clear influence of Slovenia, Austria, and Hungary. The cuisine reflects, as it were, the traces of the world politics of earlier centuries. Jota, for example, is a heavy soup made from beans, cabbage, and bacon, and comes from the mountain region of Carinthia.

In Friuli you also find *cevapcici* (Yugoslavian sausages) and goulash, as well as dumplings, strudel, and escalope. On the coast, of course, you come across Venetian fish dishes. One other typical specialty from Friuli is the delicate, air-dried San Daniele ham from the eponymous town north of Udine.

Apart from this, Friuli is also, especially in its hilly areas, a land full of wild herbs that can be used in the kitchen. Thus rocket grows pretty much everywhere, as does caraway—in the mountains, it is baked into loaves.

One very tasty meal is *pizzoccheri*, pasta made from whole-wheat and buckwheat dough. You can obtain this type of pasta in health stores. You can also make it yourself. The important thing is to sieve the buckwheat and whole-wheat flour together into a single bowl, so that the two kinds of flour mix well and absorb the necessary amount of oxygen. Apart from this, the dough is prepared in the same way as for any whole-wheat pasta—without eggs (see p. 175).

PIZZOCCHERI WITH SAGE

- INGREDIENTS (for 4 persons): 10 oz (250 g) potatoes; 12 oz (300 g) mountain cheese; 8 oz (200 g) Swiss chard; 2 cloves garlic; ¾ cup (150 g) butter; 6 sage leaves; 4 oz (100 g) freshly grated parmesan; 1 lb (400 g) buckwheat pasta.

- 1. CHOP. Peel the potatoes. Cut the potatoes and the cheese into ½ in (1 cm) cubes. Wash the chard and cut into strips. Peel the garlic and slice thinly.

- 2. COOK THE PASTA. Boil plenty of salted water in a big saucepan. Cook the potatoes for 10 minutes. Then add the buckwheat pasta. After another 10 minutes, add the chard and cook for a further 2 minutes. Pour off the water.

- 3. SWEAT THE SAGE BUTTER. Melt the butter in a saucepan, sweat the garlic thoroughly, and add the sage leaves.

- 4. LAYER. Put half the mixture of pasta and potatoes into a warm bowl. Then add the cheese cubes and cover with the rest of the pasta and potatoes.

- 5. SERVE. Pour the sage butter over the contents and sprinkle with parmesan. Alternatively, you can serve the dish on individual plates.

Pizzocheri with sage

40 min.

Tuscany, Umbria, and Marche

COOKING THAT IS SIMPLE, BUT FRESH

Peaceful hilly landscapes, slender cypress trees, and old, ruined walls. These are the images that come to mind when you think of the picture-book countryside of Tuscany. This is only one aspect of the varied scenes found in the more central areas of Italy, however: broad valleys with fertile plains alternate with thick woods and gentle olive groves. Even the rugged outline of the Apennines is part of the picture.

Everything that grows and flourishes here is turned to account in local cuisine, which uses nothing but simple and fresh ingredients (e.g., beans). The cooking tends to have the robust and indigenous quality of peasant food.

Instead of the many antipasti served in olive oil that you often find in other regions, sausage, ham, and

crostini are the usual appetizers in Tuscany. Meat is predominantly roasted—in particular poultry and game: nor should we forget the famous *bistecca alla fiorentina*, a substantial chunk of meat from white Chianina cattle that is grilled over a wood fire.

The situation is similar in the neighboring regions of Umbria and Marche. Here, too, they live off the land: wine, corn, sunflowers, olives, vegetables, and fruit are cultivated, and pigs, cattle, and sheep are bred.

As well as many popular types of sausage, Umbria can lay claim to one local specialty: black truffles that grow particularly well in the region of Norcia. Another notable dish here is *tegamaccio*, a soup made exclusively from delicious, freshwater fish—the many rivers and lakes of Umbria are swarming with them.

Naturally, there is no shortage of pasta, either. In the markets, you will often find *vin cisgrassi*, pasta filled with a ragout of chicken liver and mushrooms and baked with a topping of béchamel sauce. And in Tuscany, one favourite is *paglia e fieno* (straw and hay), a mixture of yellow and green strips of pasta with a spicy cream and mushroom sauce. The name refers only to the appearance of the dish, of course, and not its taste!

PAGLIA E FIENO

Paglia e fieno

40 min.

INGREDIENTS (serves 4–6): 4 oz (100 g) mild uncooked ham; 12 oz (300 g) fresh mushrooms (champignons, oyster mushrooms, chanterelles, or boletus); juice of ½ lemon; ½ bunch parsley; ½ bunch basil; ¾ cup (200 g) light cream; 10 tbsp (150 ml) mild meat stock; 1 clove garlic; 1½ tbsp (22 g) butter; salt; freshly ground pepper; 3½ tbsp (50 g) freshly grated parmesan; 10 oz (250 g) white ribbon pasta; 10 oz (250 g) green ribbon pasta.

1. CHOP. Cut the uncooked ham into narrow strips. Clean the mushrooms and finely slice. Drizzle the mushrooms with 1 tbsp (15 ml) lemon juice. Finely chop the parsley. Pluck the basil leaves.

2. SIMMER THE CREAM SAUCE. Melt ½ tbsp (7 g) butter in a wide-based saucepan, press the garlic clove into it, and sauté lightly. Pour in the cream and meat stock and boil down to a creamy consistency over high heat. Season with salt, pepper, and lemon juice.

3. COOK THE PASTA. Meanwhile, bring 16 cups (4 liters) salted water to a boil in a big saucepan, and cook the pasta *al dente*.

4. FRY THE MUSHROOMS. Melt 1 tbsp (15 g) butter in a skillet and fry the mushrooms, one portion at a time. Mix in the parsley and strips of ham, and fry over a low heat. Season with salt and pepper.

5. MIX. Drain the pasta well and mix loosely in a prewarmed bowl. Then pour the cream sauce over the pasta and cover with the mushroom and ham mixture. Sprinkle with basil leaves.

6. SEASON AND SERVE. Sprinkle the *paglia e fieno* with coarse ground pepper and serve with freshly grated parmesan.

Latium

DELICACIES FROM ROME

Romans prefer home cooking such as *bucatini all'amatriciana, spaghetti alla carbonara,* and *penne all'arrabiata.*

In the region around the Italian capital, people know how to make the very best of indigenous fare. This culinary skill developed as a result of the fact that Roman housewives had for centuries made a virtue of necessity: in the Eternal City, of course, the popes and aristocracy ate the fine cuts of meat, while ordinary people had to make do with the innards and less noble parts. A good example of this is *pasta alla romana,* which could be considered a typical dish of the people of Rome. Apart from this, traditions have a tendency of surviving in Rome—hardly surprising in such a historical environment. Even more than in other cities of central Italy, traditional dishes have survived here.

Apart from this, of course, Romans have no problem in adopting specialties from neighboring regions and indeed modifying them in their own way. In Latium, it is possible to make a meal out of pretty much anything.

The main thing is that these recipes are not too finicky or labor-intensive to prepare. They tend, rather, to be flavorsome and substantial. So pasta dishes in Latium are more frequently served with ewe's milk cheese—thus paying unmistakable homage to cooking in the south of Italy.

FETTUCCINE ALLA ROMANA

- INGREDIENTS (serves 4–6): for the basic sauce: 10 oz (250 g) giblets; 2 oz (50 g) streaky bacon; 1 onion; 1 carrot; 1 clove garlic; 2 cloves; 1 bay leaf; 2 tbsp (30 ml) olive oil; 2 tbsp (40 g) tomato paste; 1 cup (250 ml) white wine; salt; freshly ground pepper. In addition: 10 oz (250 g) chicken liver; 2 oz (50 g) uncooked ham; 2 tomatoes; 2 spring onions; 1 oz (20 g) dried boletus mushrooms; 3½ tbsp (50 g) freshly grated parmesan; 2 tbsp (30 g) butter; salt; ground pepper; 1 lb (400 g) fettuccine (8 pasta nests).

- 1. SOAK THE MUSHROOMS. First, soak the dried boletus mushrooms in water.

- 2. PREPARE. Cut the bacon into cubes. Finely chop the carrot and onion. Skin the tomatoes (see p. 111) and chop into small pieces. Wash the spring onion and finely chop. Cut the ham into thin strips.

- 3. COOK THE BASIC SAUCE. Put the bacon in a large skillet with the olive oil. Add the giblets to the hot bacon fat and sauté. Add the carrot and onion and

continue to sauté for a short while. Crush the garlic into the mixture and season with salt and pepper. Add the cloves and bay leaf and pour in the white wine. Simmer over low heat for about 30 minutes.

4. SEPARATE. Press the sauce through a fine-meshed sieve into a bowl to create a clear broth, or bouillon. Stir in the tomato paste and set aside.

5. SAUTÉ. Melt 1 tbsp (15 g) butter in a skillet and sauté the spring onions and ham over medium heat. Drain the mushrooms and finely chop, then add to the pan.

6. ADD THE BOUILLON AND TOMATOES. Now pour in the bouillon and simmer for about 10 minutes. Stir in the diced tomatoes and season with salt and pepper.

7. COOK THE PASTA. Meanwhile, cook the pasta *al dente* in 12 cups (3 liters) bubbling, salted water.

8. SAUTÉ THE LIVER. Chop the chicken liver into small pieces. In another skillet, melt 1 tbsp (15 g) butter and fry the pieces of liver for about 3 minutes, stirring constantly. Add salt and pepper and stir in the ham and tomato mixture.

Fettuccine alla romana

60 min.

9. SERVE. Drain the fettuccine, divide between warm plates, and pour the sauce over the pasta. Serve with freshly grated parmesan.

Sardinia

THE COOKING OF SHEPHERDS

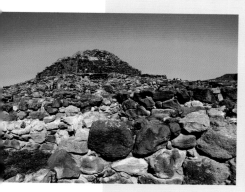

Sardinia is a sparsely inhabited island whose inhabitants have always lived on the edge of the history of Italy (and still do). Up until now, for instance, they have preserved their own language and, of course, their own style of cooking. The typical Sardinian is a shepherd and not—as you might think from the fact that Sardinia is an island—a fisherman or sailor. Hence even today the coasts are less inhabited than the inland areas.

On Sardinian feast days, the kitchen stays cold and a custom of the original Sardinian shepherd's cooking is celebrated: *arrosti* are grilled over great open fires. Lambs and kids just a few weeks old are cooked on spits to make a dish of the most delicate meat. Apart from typical festival meals such as this, the cuisine of Sardinia is very simple and tasty: soups are popular with bread, milk, meat, and even pasta. Often they are all cooked in one and the same pot and seasoned with local herbs.

The most important produce of Sardinia is, of course, ewe's milk cheese, the so-called *pecorino sardo*. There is one particularly flavorsome variant that is produced in every degree of maturity and consistency. It is also the most important element in one of the most popular pasta dishes on the island—stuffed *culingioni*.

CULINGIONI

- INGREDIENTS (serves 4–6): for the pasta: 1½ cups (200 g) flour; 1 cup (200 g) semolina; 3 eggs; salt. For the filling: 12 oz (300 g) leaf spinach; 8 oz (200 g) pecorino; 2 tbsp (30 g) butter; nutmeg; salt; freshly ground pepper. In addition: 1½ lb (500 g) ripe tomatoes; 2 tbsp (30 ml) olive oil; 3½ tbsp (50 g) freshly grated pecorino; salt; freshly ground pepper.

- 1. KNEAD THE DOUGH. Knead the flour, semolina, eggs, and a pinch of salt into a smooth dough. If the dough is too dry, mix in a little water. Then shape the dough into balls, cover with a damp dishtowel, and leave for about 30 minutes.

- 2. CHOP AND SAUTÉ THE SPINACH. For the filling of the pasta cases, clean and wash the leaf spinach and, while it is still dripping with water, place it in a hot saucepan. Let the spinach shrink and cool, press out the excess water, remove from the saucepan, and finely chop. Then briefly sauté with the butter in a skillet and season to taste with salt, pepper, and nutmeg.

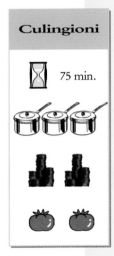

Culingioni

75 min.

3. MIX IN THE PECORINO. Cut the cheese into small pieces and mix with the spinach in a small bowl.

4. SIMMER THE TOMATO SAUCE. For the tomato sauce, skin the tomatoes (see p. 111), remove the cores and seeds, and finely chop. Then heat the olive oil in a saucepan, add the tomatoes, and leave to simmer over medium heat. Season with a little salt and pepper.

5. FILL THE PASTA CASES. Halve the dough and roll it out thinly on a work surface that has been sprinkled with flour. On one of the layers of dough place a teaspoonful of the spinach and cheese filling at intervals of about 2 in (5 cm). Carefully place the second layer of dough on top, and cut out the pasta cases with a dough cutter. Do not forget to press the edges of the *culingioni* gently down and push in with a fork all the way round so that they will stay in one piece during cooking. Leave to dry for a short while.

6. COOK. Boil 12 cups (3 liters) salted water in a large pot and add the pasta cases. After they have started to boil, reduce the heat and simmer for 7 minutes or so. Remove from the pot and drain.

7. SERVE. Divide the *culingioni* on warmed plates, pour over the tomato sauce, and sprinkle with grated pecorino. Serve straightaway.

Campania

THE HOMELAND OF PASTA AND PIZZA

In Campania, we are very close to the origins of Italian pasta—which was supposedly invented in the region of Naples. Of course, the Sicilians also claim that pasta was born on their island. Whatever the truth of the matter, the

great variety of types of pasta served in Naples and throughout Campania speaks for itself. The invention of pizza is also claimed by this region. In particular, the classic pizza margherita was created in Naples in 1889 in honor of the first Queen of Italy: with its red tomatoes, white mozzarella, and green basil, it reproduced the national colors.

The cooking of Campania is distinguished by two ingredients: cheese and vegetables. The latter led to the inhabitants of this region being given the nickname of *mangiafoglie* —"leaf-eaters." In the gardens, every conceivable kind of vegetable is grown and tended with loving care and, around Vesuvius, potatoes, fennel, artichokes, and bell peppers are all cultivated.

But the real specialty is the tomato. Tomatoes are found in Campania in the greatest profusion. From here, they spread everywhere, finally becoming popular on an international scale—for Naples is the cradle of the canned tomato industry.

Next to vegetables, cheese plays a particularly important role: types of cheese such as mozzarella, provolone and *caciocavallo*, all from this region, are essential elements in *la cucina italiana*.

As far as pasta is concerned, many of the most famous seafood dishes come from this region, since Naples, with its huge harbor, also depends on fishing for its living.

SPAGHETTI ALLE VONGOLE

■ INGREDIENTS (serves 4): 2½ lb (1 kg) fresh clams; 2 bunches flat-leaf parsley; 1 onion; 3 cloves garlic; 1 cup (250 ml) white wine; 6 tbsp (90 ml) olive oil; 2 tbsp (30 g) soft butter; 2 tbsp (30 ml) freshly squeezed lemon juice; 8 peppercorns; salt; freshly ground pepper; 1 lb (400 g) spaghetti.

■ 1. CLEAN AND COOK THE CLAMS. Wash the clams thoroughly in running water and brush them. Clams that have already opened should be discarded. Put the unopened clams in a big saucepan and boil up with the white wine.

The clams are cooked when the shells open. This usually happens after about 5 minutes. All unopened clams should be discarded. Take the rest out of the saucepan and allow them to cool. Make a bouillon by pouring the cooking liquid through a fine sieve into a bowl.

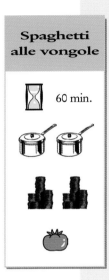

Spaghetti alle vongole

60 min.

2. CHOP. Finely chop 1 bunch parsley, the onion, and the garlic.

3. SAUTÉ AND COOK. Heat 4 tbsp (60 ml) olive oil in a saucepan and sauté the mixture of vegetables and herbs, stirring continuously. Pour in the clam bouillon and reduce by half.

4. COOK THE PASTA. Boil 16 cups (4 liters) salted water in a large saucepan and cook the spaghetti *al dente*.

5. SEASON THE CLAMS. Re-heat the clams in the sauce, but do not cook them further. Stir in the butter and season with the lemon juice, salt, and pepper.

FROM THE CAN

If you cannot obtain fresh clams, you can always use 1 lb (400 g) canned clam flesh.

6. MIX AND SERVE. Finely chop the remaining parsley and crush the peppercorns in a mortar. Drain the spaghetti and mix in 2 tbsp (30 ml) olive oil and the clam sauce. Divide between warm plates, sprinkle with parsley and crushed peppercorns, and serve.

Abruzzi, Molise, and Apulia

THE CUISINE OF PEPERONCINI

At the heel of the boot of Italy, people prefer to cook with vegetables and serve the food with plenty of bread. In addition, pasta is very popular—macaroni in particular. It does not matter which dish you are cooking, however—a couple of fresh peperoncini must always be ready for use too. They like it hot in southern Italy. These red-hot chillies are an essential ingredient of many dishes in this region. While both Abruzzi and Molise, whose smaller regions cram in landscapes of near 4,000-ft (3000-m)-high rock cliffs looming over plateaus and capes, as well as sandy beaches shimmering golden along the coasts, Apulia is if anything the opposite—here, gigantic wheat fields stretch uniformly across a great plain, and olives, grapevines, and vegetables all flourish in glorious profusion next to the wheat. Yet when it comes to cooking, these areas are, for all their difference, closely linked—thanks to the traditional grazing calendar of the shepherds, which long dictated the local lifestyle. Since the herds had to be driven to higher pastures in spring, remaining there for the summer until they were brought back down to the lowlands in the autumn, the shepherds were constantly exchanging dishes among the grazing areas. They would

cook their meals in a big cauldron, hung over an open fire on chains. Stews were a natural choice, and the recipes for these are still in use today.

The cuisine of this region is thus rather simple, with no complicated preparations or ingredients. People take what is readily available—lamb and mutton, vegetables, sheep's cheese, and pasta. Legumes such as lentils and beans are especially popular. Pasta with lentils is thus a typical delicacy of the Apulia region. A glance at the map of Italy is enough to reveal how many miles of coastline Apulia has and thus how many people depend on fishing for their livelihood. So it almost goes without saying that sea creatures of every kind are found on many menus.

PASTA E LENTICCHIE

■ INGREDIENTS (serves 6): 4 oz (100 g) streaky bacon; 4 sticks celery; 1 cup (200 g) brown lentils; ½ cup (125 ml) white wine; 1 onion; 2 cloves garlic; 4 tbsp (60 ml) olive oil; salt; freshly ground pepper; 1½ lb (600 g) fusilli.

■ 1. SOAK. Cover the lentils with water and soak overnight (12 hours).

■ 2. CHOP. On the following day, chop the bacon and onion into small cubes. Wash 2 sticks celery and cut into slices.

■ 3. SAUTÉ. Heat 1 tbsp (15 ml) olive oil in a large saucepan and sauté the bacon. Add the celery and onion and cook until glazed. Add the lentils to the saucepan, together with the water in which they have been soaked. Crush the garlic and stir into the mixture.

■ 4. COOK. Cook the lentils for about 40 minutes, until soft. Gradually add the white wine during the cooking time and, if necessary, a little water. The lentils should have a soupy consistency.

■ 5. SEASON AND SERVE. Season the lentils with salt and pepper. Cut the remaining 2 celery sticks into thin slices. Add the fusilli to the lentils, together with the celery slices. Cook for about 10 minutes. Adjust the seasoning, drizzle with 3 tbsp (45 ml) olive oil, and sprinkle with finely chopped celery leaves.

Pasta e lenticchie

 70 min.

Basilicata and Calabria

SIMPLE, MEAGER COOKING

Deep in the south of Italy, in the extended toe of Calabria, there are many places perched high on hilltops like bastions. Local inhabitants sought refuge here through the ages whenever rampaging Mediterranean peoples harried the region and made off with goods and chattel. The Calabrese people eked out an existence as shepherds, peasants, and manual workers. Even today, these regions are poor and isolated. Up until the 17th century, people were unwilling to settle on the unsafe coastal regions.

Hence the cuisine of this region is not distinguished by the way it uses the fruits of the sea, but by the fertile produce of the hilly hinterland. Here, vegetables are intensively cultivated—especially eggplants and tomatoes—as well as legumes, artichokes, bell peppers, onions, cabbage, and potatoes. Lemons and oranges also flourish here in abundance.

Macaroni with ham is a simple and typical pasta dish from Calabria. It can be made with just a few ingredients, has a certain zing thanks to the use of chillies, exhibits the typical flavor of sheep's cheese, and is given extra savor by fresh herbs and spices.

To the north lies the region of Basilicata, which in many areas is poor and isolated. It has only very few outlets to the sea. The hinterland is decidedly harsh: places such as Matera, with its stone cave dwellings and labyrinthine little alleys, are typical.

The cuisine in Matera is comprised of mostly very simple, but highly spiced, fare, since the ground here is not so fertile. Herbs are used as a good way of making up for this deficiency. So the use of peperoncini in particular is very widespread.

MACCHERONI ALLA CALABRESE

■ INGREDIENTS (serves 4): 4 oz (100 g) uncooked ham (mild variety); 2½ lb (1 kg) tomatoes; 1 bunch flat-leafed parsley; 1 bunch basil; 4 oz (100 g) caciocavallo cheese (or pecorino); 3 tbsp (45 g) shortening; 2 tbsp (30 ml) olive oil; 1 dried chili; 1 onion; 3 cloves garlic; a few black peppercorns; salt; freshly ground pepper; 1 lb (400 g) macaroni.

**Maccheroni
alla calabrese**

60 min.

1. CHOP. Blanch the tomatoes in boiling water, skin (see p. 111), remove the core and seeds, and chop the flesh. Cut the ham into strips, and finely chop the onion and garlic. Grate the *caciocavallo*, chop the parsley, and cut the basil into strips. Set the cheese and the herbs to one side. Crush the peppercorns in a mortar and also set aside.

2. SAUTÉ. In a saucepan, heat the olive oil and 1 tbsp (15 g) shortening. Sauté the onion and chili. Stir in the garlic and sauté briefly.

3. SIMMER THE SAUCE. Mix in the chopped tomato. Allow the sauce to simmer for about 30 minutes. Stir from time to time.

4. COOK THE PASTA. Boil 12 cups (3 liters) salted water in a pot, break the macaroni into pieces, and cook *al dente*.

5. SEASON. Now season the tomato sauce with salt and pepper and remove the chili. Stir in a quarter of the parsley.

6. SERVE. Drain the macaroni and place in a bowl. Mix with 2 tbsp (30 g) shortening and the crushed peppercorns. Mix in the grated cheese and the tomato sauce and sprinkle with the remaining herbs.

Sicily

THE MELTING POT OF MANY CULINARY STYLES

Sicily was always a melting pot for many peoples and their culinary styles, and this has clearly dictated the character of the local cookery—a sumptuous mixture of wonderful ingredients.

Here, Arabian aromas encounter the lush flavors of sun-ripened tomatoes; the bitter tang of wild herbs and the sweetness of oranges mingle with the sea breezes. The oil of olive trees thousands of years old is as distinctive as the piquancy of the cheese or the sweetness of honey and almonds.

Sicily is the Mediterranean's biggest island and possesses many fertile regions. Hilly and mountainous land covers about four-fifths of the total surface area. Thanks to its size, Sicily has several zones of the most varied vegetation.

The south coast is very hot, with the breezes from Africa blowing across it. As a result, almond trees in particular flourish here. The east coast lies in the protective shadow of Etna and so

is blessed by a mild climate all year round. In the west, however, it is wine that is almost exclusively cultivated. In the hilly regions, trees and plants grow that are reminiscent of the more northern latitudes: broom, walnut, and chestnut are common sights here. And on the high plateau near Etna, finally, lies Italy's granary: here, fields of corn stretch as far as the eye can see.

In short, Sicily is very well stocked with every kind of fresh ingredient: a wide variety of vegetables, olives, nuts, and—of course—citrus fruits. Tomatoes are of paramount importance and, when it comes to vegetables, the preference decidedly goes to eggplants and wild fennel. In the case of meat and cheese—and here, too, there is a rich variety from which to choose—the Sicilians have an especial liking for the produce of sheep and kids. And yet, this is far from including everything on the list of ingredients of Sicilian cuisine. Full-bodied olive oil and delicious fish—especially tuna, swordfish, and sardines—all belong to *la cucina siciliana*.

The most popular pasta dishes include pasta with sardines and fennel. In Sicily this is made with the addition of wild hill fennel, though ordinary fennel will do as well. Mixing in fish, oil, raisins, herbs, lemon, and pine nuts renders the dish typically Sicilian. Sicilians sometimes mix in tomatoes too, and broil the result with a little *caciocavallo*.

Pasta con le sarde

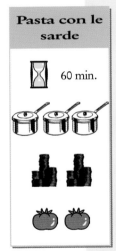

Pasta con le sarde

60 min.

■ INGREDIENTS (serves 4): 1½ lb (500 g) fresh (or canned) sardines; 1 fennel plus leaves; 1 unwaxed lemon (juice and grated rind); 1 bunch flat-leaf parsley; 4 pickled anchovy fillets; 3½ tbsp (50 g) raisins; 2 tbsp (30 g) pine nuts; 1 tsp (5 g) fennel seeds; 1 onion; 3 cloves garlic; ¾ cup (200 ml) olive oil; salt; freshly ground pepper; 1 lb (400 g) farfalle.

■ 1. PREPARE THE FISH AND SOAK THE RAISINS. Remove the heads from the sardines. Wash and dry the fish, then lightly salt, drizzle with lemon juice, and set aside. Meanwhile, soak the raisins in ½ cup (125 ml) water.

■ 2. CHOP. Clean the fennel, removing any hard bits and reserving the delicate green leaves. Boil 4 cups (1 liter) salted water in a pot, and cook the fennel for 10 minutes. Remove from the pot, drain, and cut into cubes. Reserve the cooking water. Finely chop the onion.

3. MIX THE ANCHOVY PASTE. Finely chop 1 bunch parsley. Rinse the anchovy fillets, dry, and cut into small pieces. Chop the garlic. Now grind all three ingredients in a mortar with 4 tbsp (60 ml) olive oil, the grated lemon rind, and the fennel seeds, until a paste is formed.

4. SIMMER GENTLY. Heat 2 tbsp (30 ml) olive oil in a skillet and lightly sauté the finely chopped onion until glazed. Stir in the fennel and sauté briefly. Reduce the temperature and mix together the anchovy paste, the raisins in water, 2 tbsp (30 ml) fennel broth, and the pine nuts. Simmer over low heat.

5. COOK THE PASTA. Make up the fennel cooking water to 12 cups (3 liters), salt, and bring to the boil. Add the pasta and cook *al dente*. Drain thoroughly and mix in 2 tbsp (30 ml) olive oil.

6. FRY THE SARDINES. In a second skillet, heat 4 tbsp (60 ml) olive oil. Dry the sardines on paper towels, season with salt and pepper, and fry on each side for about 2 minutes.

7. LAYER AND SERVE. Layer the pasta lengthways in a pre-warmed container and season with salt and pepper. Pour some of the anchovy sauce over each part and arrange a few sardine fillets on top. Sprinkle over coarsely chopped parsley and fennel leaves over it, and drizzle with 4 tsp (20 ml) olive oil.

Pasta from around the world

Asia

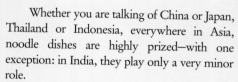

1000 YEARS OF COOKERY

One of the greatest myths about culinary history is the one claiming that European cuisine became acquainted with pasta only when Marco Polo brought it back with him from China. It is a fact, however, that noodles have been known in Asia for thousands of years—the most ancient recipe from that part of the world is a good 4000 years old.

Whether you are talking of China or Japan, Thailand or Indonesia, everywhere in Asia, noodle dishes are highly prized—with one exception: in India, they play only a very minor role.

Of course, Asian noodles are essentially quite different from the European variety. Unlike in Europe, Asian noodles are not usually made out of durum wheat or cornmeal, but from the starch of beans or rice flour. Although these taste different, they are generally similar to their European cousins in appearance. Most Asian noodles have the shape of thin spaghetti.

THE MOST IMPORTANT ASIAN NOODLE TYPES

- GLASS NOODLES: the type that is particularly popular in China is mainly made from mung beans, but partly also out of soybeans or tapioca starch. The type that is also known by the name of "cellophane" noodles is not cooked, but scalded in boiling water. It should then be simmered for a good 10 minutes in hot water. Drain the long noodles and cut them into smaller pieces with scissors before serving.

- MIE NOODLES: these noodles made of wheat flour are like spaghetti, but are wrapped up into a ball. They can also be made out of eggs, as well as from pure wheat dough. They are also flavored by their different contents—e.g., shrimp or fish. They are often commercially available ready-made: just scald them and allow them to cook for 2 minutes.

- RICE NOODLES: these noodles, which are popular in many different parts of Asia, are produced from rice flour—so they fully deserve their name. Depending on their origin, they can either be as thin as spaghetti or as broad as ribbon noodles. These, too, are not cooked in salted water, but simply have hot water poured over them and are then allowed to cook for a few minutes.

■ UNO NOODLES: these noodles, widespread in Japan, are prepared from wheat flour and—like European types of noodle—cooked in salted water. The thin noodles thereupon swell up and turn white. They are served in particular with salads and soups.

■ SOBA NOODLES: this Japanese noodle specialty consists of buckwheat and portions of wheat: it is prepared in the same way as uno noodles. As soba noodles have a stronger taste, however, they are not as a rule served with salads or soups, but as an accompaniment to meat and fish dishes.

■ WONTON DOUGH: these dough cases made of corn, eggs, and water are like lasagna; they are cooked and filled in exactly the same way.

Methods of preparation

As in Europe, there are countless noodle and pasta recipes in Asia, all of them varying considerably from country to country and region to region. So there is no uniform or typical mode of preparation or serving.

Unlike the culinary customs prevalent in Italy, there are many recipes with cold noodles, as is the case with, for example, Chinese mie noodles. The noodles are prepared in a way that suits this—as a rule they are scalded or steamed. They are then left to cool and served either as a side dish or in salads.

Other ways of preparing noodles include frying and deep-frying. In the latter case, for example, the noodles are dipped for a few minutes into hot soy-oil and served immediately.

One classic Chinese mode of preparation is steaming over a wok. For this you will need, as well as your wok, a cheap steaming basket of bamboo. Fill the bottom of the wok with water and bring to a boil. Place the steaming basket filled with noodles in the wok, and leave to simmer.

TYPICAL INGREDIENTS

These days, wherever you are in the world, Asian shops can supply all the important ingredients for the preparation of Asian noodle recipes. Many of them are also available over the internet.

Of particular importance are typical vegetables such as bamboo and soybeans, mu-err and shiitake mushrooms, and seaweed and water chestnuts. The taste comes in particular from the various herbs and spices used. Only a few of them are current in Europe—curry and cumin, turmeric and ginger, as well as Thai basil, lemon grass, and the roots of the galanga (or Thai ginger) plant.

The dishes are often spiced with different types of sauce and other liquids. So Asian cooking is unthinkable without soy and fish sauce, or indeed sesame oil. In addition, in various regions you will find coconut milk, rice vinegar, and rice wine.

One particularity is the availability of various pastes, especially the most diverse curry mixtures: there are also bean and shrimp pastes, and the well-known *sambal oelek*.

Germany, Austria, and Switzerland

Side dishes and salads

As in Italy, the cuisines of Germany, Austria, and Switzerland are unthinkable without noodle and pasta dishes. Unlike in the motherland of pasta, however, where spaghetti is eaten as an independent dish, either as an appetizer or main course, in German-speaking countries noodles are traditionally served as an accompaniment to meat and fish dishes.

In addition, there are countless salads that are served with fresh vegetables and cold noodles. These enjoy particular popularity at parties, where they are a traditional component of the buffet table.

Noodles here made their great breakthrough thanks to the great trading houses of the 16th century. Since then, noodles and pasta have celebrated a ceaseless, triumphal procession. These days, in German-speaking areas, there is an incredibly large range of noodles to try.

Next to the well-known Italian types of pasta, such as spaghetti and macaroni, which have long since conquered the shelves of supermarkets, many homegrown specialties also enjoy great popularity. Especially large is the choice of pasta and noodles made from eggs, that in German-speaking lands reflects a long tradition. Depending on their content, you can speak of egg noodles (with 1 egg per pound/2 eggs per kilo of semolina); noodles with high egg content (at least 2 eggs per pound/4 eggs per kilo); and noodles with very high egg content (3 eggs per pound/6 eggs per kilo).

DESIGNER NOODLES: A NEW TREND

The German noodle industry has long offered more than the traditional products. The wide selection available is distinguished by original and daring noodle creations. Noodles that are colored and flavored in unusual fashions have conquered the market. The range extends from noodles flavored with green spinach or bear's garlic, to those with red colorings, e.g., from beets or red wine, to ones with chocolate flavoring. Creativity is even shown in the development of new shapes: the classics include tiny noodles in the shape of letters of the alphabet, which every child knows and loves in the form of alphabet soup. Among the newer creations we find noodles in little heart shapes, or even with Christmas motifs. The trend is moving toward designer noodles that are very much in the public eye and made to appeal to young and fashion-conscious customers. So there is a continuous stream of new products, in the most original shapes, coming onto the market.

REGIONAL SPECIALTIES

Especially in southern Germany, but also in Austria and Switzerland, many noodle specialties are known. The best-known and best-loved specialties in the entire German-speaking realm are *Swabian Spätzle:* thick, homemade egg noodles that go superbly well with heavy sauces and meat dishes.

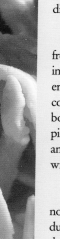

Spätzle taste best when they are made fresh: "scraped from the board" as they say in Swabia. This needs to be taken quite literally: the soft dough made from eggs, cornmeal, and salt is laid on a kitchen board and from there scraped in little pieces directly into boiling, salted water. As an alternative, *Spätzle* can be produced with a special plane.

In Austria, homemade variants of the noodle are called *Nockerln*, similar to small dumplings. In order to make these, an egg dough is prepared—it must not be too runny. Here, too, we find a noodle "plane" being used, called (naturally enough) a "dumpling plane." But the dough can also be pressed through a sieve. If you can, add a little nutmeg to the dough—this gives the dumplings their special flavor.

The basic recipe for *Spätzle* or *Nockerln* is in many regions developed into weird and wonderful variants. For instance, cheese *Spätzle* are popular: grated cheese (e.g., Emmental) and finely chopped onions are worked into the dough.

Among the highlights of southern German cooking we also find the so-called Swabian ravioli: pasta cases filled with minced meat and leek, and served in a broth with fried onion rings.

The list of favorite noodle dishes includes, last but not least, the most varied noodle soups and puddings. The latter are not only very popular when baked with béchamel sauce or cheese, but in sweet variants: e.g., with fruit.

Steamed noodles

Steamed noodles, so popular in Austria in particular, are in fact not noodles at all, but a kind of dumpling made from yeast dough, which is often enjoyed with fruity and sweet sauces as a dessert.

Picture credits

Techniker Krankenkasse: 25
Teigwaren Riesa GmbH, Nudelcenter Riesa: 32-33, 44 o.
Villeroy & Boch AG, Mettlach: 39, 214
WMF AG, Geislingen/Steige: 71-73, 84-85, 87

We are grateful to the following for their friendly support:

ASA SELECTION Wohnaccessoires Handels GmbH, Höhr-
    Grenzhausen
Bos Food GmbH, Meerbusch
Birkel Teigwaren GmbH, Weinheim
Herrmann GmbH Teigwaren-Spezialitäten, Kirchheim/Teck
Küchenprofi GmbH & Co. KG, Solingen
Mamma Lucia, Eterna Nahrungsmittel GmbH, Frankfurt/Main
Teigwaren Riesa GmbH, Nudelcenter Riesa

Culinary advice and cooking: Roger Kimpel

With the collaboration of: Yara Hackstein, Carola Struck,
    Susanne Gilsbach, and Mathias Hinkerode.

List of recipes

General index